W9-DDK-193

RAISING
THE BAR
MISSIONARIES TO MATCH THE MESSAGE

OTHER BOOKS AND BOOKS ON CASSETTE
BY ED J. PINEGAR:

The Ultimate Missionary Companion

Latter-day Commentary on the Old Testament

Lengthen Your Shuffle

Latter-day Commentary on the New Testament

Leadership for Saints

TALK TAPES BY ED J. PINEGAR:

Preparing the Lord's Missionary

After Your Mission

Hope in Christ

Overcoming Twelve Tough Temptations

Power Tools for Missionaries

Preparing for a Mission

Turn It Over to the Lord

RAISING THE BAR

MISSIONARIES TO MATCH THE MESSAGE

ED J. PINEGAR

Covenant Communications, Inc.

Cover design copyrighted 2003 by Covenant Communications, Inc.

Published by Covenant Communications, Inc.
American Fork, Utah

Copyright © 2003 by Ed J. Pinegar
All rights reserved. No part of this book may be reproduced in any format or in any medium without
the written permission of the publisher, Covenant Communications, Inc., P.O. Box 416, American
Fork, UT 84003. The views expressed herein are the responsibility of the author and do not necessarily
represent the position of Covenant Communications, Inc.

Printed in Canada
First Printing: October 2003

08 07 06 05 04 03   10 9 8 7 6 5 4 3 2 1

ISBN 1-59156-338-0

DEDICATION

To all the Lord's disciples who labor diligently
to build up the kingdom of God.
May you be blessed forever.

ACKNOWLEDGEMENTS

Thank you to my sweetheart Pat, my eternal and missionary companion, with whom I have shared so many wonderful missionary experiences with.

Also, with deep appreciation for all of the missionaries I have served with and Church leaders who have taught me. Grateful appreciation to Covenant Communications, especially Shauna Humphreys and Angela Colvin, who were simply magnificent in their editorial work.

In addition, I would like to thank those unknown authors whose words have inspired the honest in heart. After thirty years of teaching and having been intimately involved in missionary work, I have collected many wonderful thoughts and quotes from Church leaders, fellow teachers, missionaries, and students. I am indebted to them and their goodness. Unfortunately, it is sometimes nearly impossible to obtain the original sources for some of these inspiring quotes—so many wonderful things have been produced and created with no name attached. And though we have searched diligently to find every source possible to give credit where credit is due, where a name could not be found, we would like to acknowledge that lives will be blessed by such wonderful unknown authors. Thank you.

TABLE OF CONTENTS

INTRODUCTION

The purpose of missionary work is to bring souls to Christ. As a missionary or prospective missionary, you are to prepare yourself to become a worthy instrument in the hands of the Lord. You will be acting as His ambassador—even the Savior's representative. To prepare to do this requires effort. This book can help you "raise the bar" in your level of worthiness and desire, helping you to prepare well and become a pure disciple of Jesus Christ.

Like all things that are worthwhile, such preparation requires faith, diligence, patience, perseverance, and commitment. As you proceed through the book, you will begin to become the kind of missionary that the Lord wants you to be. Remember, you will be blessed as you prepare to serve the Lord with all your heart, might, mind, and strength.

One of the most important parts of preparing for your mission is catching the vision of the work—it will motivate you to prepare every needful thing. Understanding the worth of souls and the importance of this work in our own lives, the destiny of the kingdom of God, and the lives of our brothers and sisters is paramount to having a successful mission. This letter describes how one missionary came to understand this, and how that vision strengthened her testimony of missionary work and how to be successful at it.

April 9, 1990

Dear President Pinegar,

I want to thank you for telling us to open our mouths in the departure meeting. I know the Lord has commanded us to do so for a purpose and I would like to share an experience with you.

My first Sunday here in Paraguay, we rode a bus to a nearby town for a discussion. I was sitting next to a woman and felt the need to talk to her and give her a Book of Mormon. And though I was only in the field four days and was afraid to speak because of my lack of language experience, the Lord blessed me with the words and the ability to understand her. I gave her the Book of Mormon and, with the help of my companion, got her address.

The elders found her home and challenged her to be baptized in the first discussion, which she accepted. What a beautiful feeling it was to see her at church and know the Lord had used me as an instrument in His hands, even in my rough form. Tell the missionaries to open their mouths right away. Don't wait until you feel comfortable with the language. Many precious souls may be lost if you wait. Every soul is important to Heavenly Father and He will bless you by the Holy Ghost to accomplish His purposes.

The gospel of Jesus Christ is once again on the earth in its complete form. And I'm grateful I can help share it.

May God continue to bless you in all you do.

Sister Kerrie Cross
Paraguay Asuncion Mission

"Many precious souls may be lost if you wait. Every soul is important to Heavenly Father and He will bless you by the Holy Ghost to accomplish His purposes." This testimony, brothers and sisters, is one she gained before entering the field—it was merely strengthened when she saw the fruits of her labors. She was prepared with obedience, faith, her own testimony of the Book of Mormon, and a vision of the work.

President Ezra Taft Benson has emphasized four things to help you prepare to be a successful missionary as well.

I testify to you of the truthfulness of these four great points of emphasis on missionary work . . . First, the sacredness of saving souls and the importance of greatly increasing the number of convert baptisms. Second, the necessity of increasing our own personal faith in order that convert baptisms will increase in a significant and dramatic way. Third, the importance of missionaries prayerfully . . . setting personal convert baptismal goals. Fourth, the urgency of being actively and productively engaged in member-missionary work in order that the Lord's harvest may be accomplished.

(Ezra Taft Benson,
"President Kimball's Vision of Missionary Work," *Ensign*, July 1985, 11.)

As we examine these four concepts in depth, remember to do your part in preparation. The Lord is always ready to do His. As you prepare, you will not fear, and the Lord will give you the strength you need to succeed.

CHAPTER 1
PROCLAIMING THE GOSPEL

The Lord, through the holy scriptures, has spoken. We are to proclaim His gospel to all people in all lands. Consider the following scriptures:

- "Go ye therefore, and teach all nations, baptizing them in the name of the Father, and of the Son, and of the Holy Ghost: Teaching them to observe all things whatsoever I have commanded you: and, lo, I am with you alway, even unto the end of the world. Amen" (Matt. 28:18–20).
- "Go ye into all the world, and preach the gospel to every creature" (Mark 16:15).
- "Repentance and remission of sins should be preached . . . among all nations" (Luke 24:47).
- "For behold, thus said Jesus Christ, the Son of God, unto his disciples who should tarry, yea, and also to all his disciples, in the hearing of the multitude: Go ye into all the world, and preach the gospel to every creature" (Morm. 9:22).
- "For verily the voice of the Lord is unto all men, and there is none to escape; and there is no eye that shall not see, neither ear that shall not hear, neither heart that shall not be penetrated. And the voice of warning shall be unto all people, by the mouths of my disciples, whom I have chosen in these last days" (D&C 1:2, 4).
- "Send forth the elders of my church unto the nations which are afar off; unto the islands of the sea; send forth unto foreign lands; call upon all nations, first upon the Gentiles, and then upon the Jews" (D&C 133:8).

The Savior has made it abundantly clear that we are to take His gospel and proclaim it to every nation, every land, every people, every tongue, every soul, every creature—all the world. We are to preach His word and "stand as witnesses of God at all times and in all things and in all places" (Mosiah 18:8–9). The prophets have taught us this concept through the ages.

Not only does scripture make the Lord's feelings about missionary work clear, but He has chosen to reemphasize the importance of it time after time through His modern prophets. Ponder each of the following quotes in order to catch the vision of the work as our Church leaders have. Our beloved prophet, Gordon B. Hinckley, admonishes us:

> I wish I could awaken in the heart of every man, woman, boy, and girl here this morning the great consuming desire to share the gospel with others. If you do that you live better, you try to make your lives more exemplary because you know that those you teach will not believe unless you back up what you say by the goodness of your lives. Nobody can foretell the consequences of that which you do when you teach the gospel to another. Missionary work is a work of love and trust, and it has to be done on that basis. Be a part of this great process which constantly adds to the vitality of the Church. Every time a new member comes into the Church, something happens. There is an infusion of strength and faith and testimony that is wonderful. Think of what this Church would be without the missionary program. Think of it! I think this is the greatest age in the history of the world. I think this is the greatest time in the history of the Church. I believe that. I think there will be greater times in the future. We are growing ever and ever stronger. . . . What a responsibility we have. The whole fate of the world depends on us, according to the revelations of the Almighty. We cannot waste time. We cannot be unrighteous in our living. We cannot let our thoughts dwell on immoral things. We have to be the very best that we can be, you and I, because the very relationship of God our Eternal Father to His children on the earth depends on their accepting what we have come to teach according to His magnificent word.
>
> (Gordon B. Hinckley, *Teachings of Gordon B. Hinckley* [Salt Lake City: Deseret Book, 1997], 374.)

The Prophet Joseph has declared: "After all that has been said, the greatest and most important duty is to preach the Gospel" (Joseph Smith, *History of The Church of Jesus Christ of Latter-day Saints*, 2nd ed., hereafter cited as *HC* [Salt Lake City: Deseret Book, 1980], 2:478).

President Benson exhorts, saying:

> As members of the Lord's Church, we must take missionary work more seriously. The Lord's commission to "preach the gospel to every creature" (Mark 16:15) will never change in our dispensation. We have been greatly blessed with the material means, the technology, and an inspired message to bring the gospel to all men. More is expected of us than any previous generation. Where "much is given much is required" (D&C 82:3).
>
> ("Our Responsibility to Share the Gospel," *Ensign*, May 1985, 6.)

He also quotes previous Church Presidents as teaching similar principles:

> Our members need to understand their responsibility to do missionary work and then do it. I fully endorse the words of President Spencer W. Kimball: "Do we really believe in revelation? Then why cannot we accept fully as the revealed word of God the revelation of the prophet, President David O. McKay, wherein he brought to the Church and to the world this valuable Church slogan, "Every member a missionary"? How else could the Lord expect to perform His work except through the Saints who have covenanted to serve Him? You and I have made such a covenant. Will we honor our sacred covenant?
>
> (Ezra Taft Benson, *The Teachings of Ezra Taft Benson*, comp. Reed Benson [Salt Lake City: Bookcraft, 1988], 208.)

President Joseph F. Smith has also reminded us:

> There can be no greater or more important calling for man than that in which the Elders of The Church of Jesus Christ of Latter-day Saints are engaged when in the discharge of their

duties as missionaries to the world. They stand as teachers, counselors and leaders to the people. They are commissioned with the word of life, and "the power of God unto salvation," to minister unto this proud, conceited, self-righteous, but benighted and degenerate world.

("The Sacredness of Our Calling," *Millennial Star*, 28 June 1875, 408.)

President John Taylor clearly stated our mission. He said:

Our mission has principally been to preach the first principles of the gospel, calling upon men everywhere to believe in the Lord God of heaven, he that created the heavens and the earth, the seas, and the fountains of waters; to believe in his Son, Jesus Christ, repenting of their sins, to be baptized for the remission of the same; and then we have promised them the Holy Ghost. In doing this the Lord has stood by us, sustaining those principles that we have advanced; and when we have ministered unto men the ordinances of the gospel; they have received for themselves the witness of the Spirit, even the Holy Ghost, making known to them for a surety that the principles that they had received were from God.

(*The Gospel Kingdom*, sel. G. Homer Durham
[Salt Lake City: Bookcraft, 1943], 223.)

David O. McKay has said:

Ours is the responsibility—greater than ever before:

To proclaim that the Church was divinely established by the appearance of God the Father and his Son Jesus Christ to the Prophet Joseph Smith, and that divine authority through the priesthood is given to represent Deity in establishing Christ's Church upon the earth.

To proclaim that its assigned responsibility to fulfill the admonition of Jesus to his Apostles: "Go ye therefore, and teach all nations, baptizing them in the name of the Father, and of the Son, and of the Holy Ghost: Teaching them to observe all things whatsoever I have commanded you: and, lo, I am with you alway, even unto the end of the world. Amen" (Matt. 28:19–20).

To proclaim peace and goodwill unto all mankind.

To exert every effort and all means within our reach to make evil-thinking men good, and good men better, and all people happier.

To proclaim the truth that each individual is a child of God and important in his sight . . .

We are all missionaries. We may drop a word here, bear our testimony, be an exemplar by what we do; and, as we accept this call and discharge our duties in the stakes, wards, quorums, and the mission field, our acts will "roll from soul to soul and go forever and forever."

(Conference Report, hereafter cited as CR, Oct. 1969, 86–87)

Finally, Heber J. Grant taught us: "The missionary work of the Latter-day Saints is the greatest of all the great works in all the world" (CR, Oct. 1921, 5).

We must never forget. This is our duty as we are charged with pruning the vineyard for the last time (see Jacob 5:70–77; D&C 138:56). The work will go forth in the strength and power of the Lord. The Prophet Joseph Smith has prophesied of this:

Our missionaries are going forth to different nations, and in Germany, Palestine, New Holland, Australia, the East Indies, and other places, the Standard of Truth has been erected; no unhallowed hand can stop the work from progressing; persecutions may rage, mobs may combine, armies may assemble, calumny may defame, but the truth of God will go forth boldly, nobly, and independent, till it has penetrated every continent, visited every clime, swept every country, and sounded in every ear, till the purposes of God shall be accomplished, and the Great Jehovah shall say the work is done.

(*HC*, 4:540.)

It is up to us whether we will be part of that great work, or impede it.

CONCLUSION

One can see that our duty is clear—to invite all mankind to come unto Christ that they might enjoy the blessings of exaltation. We are to proclaim the gospel, perfect the Saints, and redeem the dead. This is all part of the great plan of happiness. This work is a grave responsibility, and the Lord needs those who preach His gospel to be more than prepared; they must be worthy, willing, and eager to serve. It is our sacred calling as disciples of Jesus Christ to help our brothers and sisters come unto Him.

CHAPTER 2
CATCHING THE VISION

Probably the best scriptural summary of what the Lord's servants should be and do is found in Doctrine and Covenants, section 4. The words of this revelation are inspirational and instructional. Never have seven short verses had such a profound effect on hundreds of thousands of missionaries. I have watched missionaries as they have read, recited, and pondered those precious words, and prayed to have the strength to live them. Surely Alma was right: "The preaching of the word had a great tendency to lead the people to do that which was just" (Alma 31:5). There is virtue and power in the word of God, and Doctrine and Covenants, section 4, exemplifies that principle every day throughout the world in the lives of the Lord's disciples. I have seen missionaries with testimonies in their souls and tears in their eyes as this scripture becomes part of their lives. Remember that this scripture applies to all the facets of service as we seek to build up the kingdom of God. It is the standard by which all Saints should live. As we qualify ourselves for the work (bringing souls to Christ) we hopefully take upon ourselves the divine nature of Christ (see 2 Pet. 1:3–12). These divine attributes will not only qualify us for the work but will bring about our transformation into being like the Lord Jesus Christ (see Moro. 7:48; 3 Ne. 27:27).

THE SCRIPTURES CLEAR OUR VISION

I encourage you to read and reread section 4 of the Doctrine and Covenants. It will cultivate your desire to serve, which will motivate you to become the missionary the Lord wants you to be.

D&C 4:1—A Marvelous Work

Think of the wording the Lord uses here. A *marvelous* work. The Book of Mormon is a marvelous work. It is a marvelous work and a wonder. But it was merely the beginning of the Restoration of the fullness of times. Everything about the Restoration is marvelous: the gospel was restored through the Book of Mormon; the priesthood was restored through John the Baptist, Peter, James, and John; the Church and kingdom were then restored, and with that came all the blessings of the temple and priesthood keys that would allow the Lord's kingdom to be here again upon the earth; we understand who we are, where we came from, and what we can become; and we know we have a Heavenly Father who hears us and loves us. Is not this amazing, awe inspiring, and *marvelous*? Indeed this is a marvelous work and a wonder that has come forth. As we begin to understand—to see and marvel at the gospel for what it is—how can we help wanting to share it with all of God's children?

D&C 4:2—Serve God with All Your Heart, Might, Mind and Strength

With all our heart. When we serve with all our heart, it means we love God—we love our fellowmen. Our affection for the Lord and His work is evident. We will *want* to do His will because we've yielded our hearts unto God (see Hel. 3:35). We will love God and His children so much we will want to spread the gospel.

With all our might means with all of our willpower, our desire, and our efforts. We concentrate on the things of the Lord. We are completely invested in what the Lord would have us do. We give it our all.

With all our mind is with all our mental capacities, our reasoning abilities, our understanding, and our intellectual powers. Our mind is on the things of the Lord. We are truly focusing ourselves on the work of the Lord—with an eye single to the glory of God.

With all our strength means we give everything to the Lord. We literally put all of our physical powers and our mental, emotional, and spiritual strength in all things the Lord would have us do. Every fiber of our being is focused on His work.

Yes, to be the missionaries the Lord expects us to be, we must serve Him with *all* our heart, might, mind, and strength. With this complete and unwavering devotion to God, we will desire to serve. A mission becomes something we anticipate and love, not merely wait out. When we turn all our capacity over to the Lord, He can do greater things with us than we could ever do alone.

D&C 4:2—That We May Stand Blameless

Joseph Fielding Smith said:

> The preaching of the Gospel should be done in the spirit of the utmost humility and perseverance. Missionaries are commanded not to idle away their time, but to give to the Lord their heart, and serve him with all their "might, mind and strength." Every missionary who goes forth is under the solemn obligation and pledge to bear testimony of the restoration of the Gospel, and witness of its truth. In doing this, he leaves all who hear him without excuse and their sins are on their own heads. If he fails to do this then he will not "stand blameless before God at the last day."
>
> (Joseph Fielding Smith, *Church History
> and Modern Revelation,* 4 vols. [Salt Lake City:
> The Church of Jesus Christ of Latter-day Saints, 1946–1949], 1:v.)

Not only are you free of others' sins, but it is interesting to note that we become blameless, guiltless, free from our own sin as we serve: "Your sins are forgiven you, and you shall be laden with sheaves upon your back, for the laborer is worthy of his hire" (D&C 31:5). Part of repentance is dedicating our lives to the Lord. It is not merely forsaking, it's *doing.* When we confess and forsake our sins we go forward in righteousness. For example, when Enos was praying for forgiveness and his guilt was swept away, his heart then turned to the welfare of the Nephites, then to the Lamanites and to future people who would be upon this continent that they might receive the gospel and the record of his people. You see, when you stand blameless, because you are free from sin, the Spirit is upon you and you have an overwhelming desire to do good, so you immediately turn to doing the Lord's will by seeking to bless and serve others. Similarly, when you seek to serve and bless, you no longer desire anything evil, and so you repent more and become more blameless. We can see that when we thrust in our sickle and work with all our heart, might, mind, and soul, working hard and smart, our sins are forgiven. It is interesting to note that in the Epistle of James, 5:20, the Lord says, "Let him know, that he which converteth the sinner from the error of his way shall save a soul from death, and shall hide a multitude of sins." As we help people come into the kingdom, we become purified. We become true disciples of the Lord Jesus Christ and free from sin.

D&C 4:3—If You Have Desires to Serve God Ye Are Called

Desire surely is the beginning. Many things create desire. We have the desire to serve because we love God; because we love our fellowmen; because we're grateful for the Atonement of our Savior Jesus Christ; because we have a desire to help people be happy; because we understand the nature of the eternal plan of God—the plan of happiness; because we come to understand the depth of the gospel of Jesus Christ as it is centered in the Atonement; because when we understand any of the principles and doctrines of the gospel, our desire to share them with others will increase. Notice how the sons of Mosiah felt regarding this: "Now they were desirous that salvation should be declared to every creature, for they could not bear that any human soul should perish; yea, even the very thoughts that any soul should endure endless torment did cause them to quake and tremble" (Mosiah 28:3).

As our conversion deepens, our faith in and love of God raises the desire within us to serve. We will want everyone to feel what we feel, and know what we know.

D&C 4:4—The Field Is White Already to Harvest

There had been a long, dark time on the planet Earth prior to the Restoration of the gospel of Jesus Christ, but times have changed. The field is now white, ready to harvest. There are so many who want and need the gospel, so many you can reach. You are called to declare His word throughout the earth even as Mormon recorded: "Behold, I am a disciple of Jesus Christ, the Son of God. I have been called of him to declare his word among his people, that they might have everlasting life" (3 Ne. 5:13).

The elect will hear the word of God: "And ye are called to bring to pass the gathering of mine elect; for mine elect hear my voice and harden not their hearts" (D&C 29:7). We can see now that there will be, and are, elect sons and daughters of God who will hear His voice and will not harden their hearts. They will come unto Christ as we love them and teach them by the Spirit, that they might come to know the truth.

D&C 4:5—Qualifying for the Work

The Lord expects us to be full of faith, hope, charity, and love, with an eye single to the glory of God. This is what qualifies us for the work. Through our faith we develop a relationship with the Lord and want to serve Him. We gain hope in eternal life; we have the vision of what we are doing here. Finally, we develop a Christlike love that prompts us to want to share all this with all of God's children. Let's discuss how to qualify for the work. To do so we must obtain the following:

Faith. Faith is the first principle of the gospel of Jesus Christ, the governing principle in applying the Atonement to our life. We learn that it is impossible to please God except with faith (see Heb. 11:6). Faith, then, becomes that which we must possess not only in order to gain eternal life, but also to do the will of God while we are on the earth. In Hebrews 11 and Alma 32, we learn that faith is something we hope for, yet do not see. Too often we end our definition of faith with this hopeful and believing stage. The Prophet Joseph Smith went on in the *Lectures on Faith* to describe the three degrees of faith. The first degree is the substance of things hoped for (see *Lectures on Faith* 1:7–8). Of the second degree, the Prophet Joseph said, "Faith is the moving cause of all action in intelligent beings" (*Lectures on Faith* 1:12). The third degree of faith is the principle and source of power (see *Lectures on Faith* 1:15). When all three degrees are applied, faith is exercised to its fullest. The Prophet went on to say, "Faith, then, is the first great governing principle which has power, dominion, and authority over all things; by it they exist, by it they are upheld, by it they are changed or by it they remain agreeable to the will of God" (*Lectures on Faith* 1:24).

Is our faith sufficient now? In Luke we read: "And the apostles said unto the Lord, Increase our faith" (Luke 17:5). If the Apostles of the Lord needed an increase in faith, how much more do we need greater faith in our lives, especially if we are to be missionaries!

Faith can do all things according to the will of God. In our lives the most important thing we will ever do is to repent and come unto Christ with full purpose of heart. The thing that will be of most worth to us and bring us true joy is to help others repent (see D&C 15:6; 18:10–16; Alma 29:9–10). Amulek taught:

> And thus he shall bring salvation to all those who shall believe on his name; this being the intent of this last sacrifice, to bring about the bowels of mercy, which overpowereth justice, and bringeth about means unto men that they may have faith unto repentance. And thus mercy can satisfy the demands of justice, and encircles them in the arms of safety, while he that exercises no faith unto repentance is exposed to the whole law of the demands of justice; therefore only unto him that has faith unto repentance is brought about the great and eternal plan of redemption. Therefore may God grant unto you, my brethren, that ye may begin to exercise your faith unto repentance, that ye begin to call upon his holy name, that he would have mercy upon you."
>
> (Alma 34:15–17.)

The prophets have made it clear that we must exercise faith in the Lord Jesus Christ, and they have explained what that means in our daily lives. President Benson has said:

> Now let me describe to you what faith in Jesus Christ means. Faith in Him is more than mere acknowledgment that He lives. It is more than professing belief. Faith in Jesus Christ consists of complete reliance on Him. As God, He has infinite power, intelligence, and love. There is no human problem beyond His capacity to solve. Because He descended below all things, He knows how to help us rise above our daily difficulties.
>
> (*The Teachings of Ezra Taft Benson*, 66.)

President Hinckley reminds us:

> If there is any one thing you and I need in this world it is faith, that dynamic, powerful, marvelous element by which, as Paul declared, the very worlds were framed (Heb. 11:3). . . . Faith—the kind of faith that moves one to get on his knees and plead with the Lord and then get on his feet and go to work—is an asset beyond compare, even in the acquisition of secular knowledge.
>
> (*Teachings of Gordon B. Hinckley*, 186.)

Here are some things to remember concerning faith and how we can increase it in our lives.

• Faith is a doctrine of power. Examples from scripture and revelation:

1. The earth was created by the power of faith (see Heb. 11:3). It is no wonder that the Lord has raised the bar. Look at how much faith can do! Could we ever truly serve Him without our faith?
2. The power of the priesthood is faith (see Thorpe B. Isaacson, CR, Apr. 1954, 126).
3. Faith is the foundation of all righteousness (see *Lectures on Faith* 1:10).
4. The powers of the priesthood are inseparably connected with the powers of heaven, and can be worked only through the principles of righteousness (see D&C 121:36).
5. Faith is an attribute of God and dwells independently in Him (see *Lectures on Faith* 2:2).

• Just men and women live by faith (see Hab. 2:4; Gal. 3:11; and Rom. 1:16). Examples from scripture:

1. Just men are made perfect (see D&C 76:69).
2. We are justified by our faith by the Spirit through the grace of our Savior Jesus Christ and His atoning sacrifice (see Rom. 3:28, 5:1).

• Faith is a power and blessings in our lives. Examples from scripture:

1. Faith is the shield of protection from the fiery darts of the adversary (see Eph.6:16).
2. Faith is evidenced by our works (see James 2:18).
3. Enos, the great prophet, exercised faith unto repentance, and his guilt was swept away (see Enos 1:8).
4. By faith the prophet Lehi received the blessing and the gift of the Holy Ghost (1 Ne. 10:17).
5. Living by the Spirit comes from faith (see 1 Ne. 10:17).
6. Prayers to heal the sick, as well as miracles, occur by the power of faith (see James 5:15; 2 Ne. 26:13).
7. The Liahona worked by faith, diligence, and giving heed to the word (see 1 Ne. 16:28).
8. Receiving direction in life depends on the faith we exercise (see Alma 37:40–44).
9. Faith gives us strength and it can do all things. (see Alma 2:30, 14:26).
10. We are alive in Christ through faith (see 2 Ne. 25:25).
11. We become mighty in word, able to preach the word through faith in the Lord Jesus Christ (see Ether 12:23).
12. Miracles are wrought through faith; angels appear through faith on the Lord Jesus Christ (Moro. 3:37).
13. We learn through faith (see D&C 88:118).
14. By faith we can do all things that are expedient in the Lord (see 2 Ne. 1:10; Moro. 7:33).
15. We pray, exercising faith with real intent for help with struggling children, and the Lord will send angels (see Mosiah 27:13–14), be they mortal or celestial.
16. It was faith that Nephi and Lehi (the sons of Helaman) exercised to help bring about the great change among the Lamanites (see Ether 12:14).
17. Faith is necessary in order that the Lord can work through us, for He works only with those who exercise faith (see Ether 12:30).
18. Faith is the principle that moves us to do good (see Alma 29:4).

When the first elders were taught in the School of the Prophets they were taught seven lectures on faith. This was their preparation to serve as missionaries—increasing their faith. We too can increase our faith. Let's not move all the mountains today. Let's just have faith to follow the prophets and prepare ourselves to be servants of the Lord Jesus Christ to become missionaries to match the message. Let's have faith enough to build up the kingdom of God through love and service to our fellow beings. By small and simple things, great things come to pass—simply through exercising our faith (see D&C 64:33). So let us commit to some goals and a plan to increase our faith by searching the scriptures, fasting and prayer, and being full of humility that we might teach our brothers and sisters to increase their faith in coming unto Christ.

Hope. Hope is the next principle we should explore in learning to qualify for the work. Our anticipation and expectation for things to be good or better in our lives is called hope. Our hope is based upon the Lord Jesus Christ, the plan of happiness, and eternal life, which God promised to the faithful before the world began (see Titus 1:2). Hope provides us with a sense of confidence as we look forward to life in righteousness. When we lose hope, life becomes difficult in every sense. We then fail to enjoy life or attempt to do anything to build a better future. A life without hope is empty; but a life filled with hope is a life filled with light and meaning. We can start with faith in Jesus Christ and the gospel plan, and an attitude of being realistically optimistic.

Hope is centered in Christ. Through Christ we can obtain a forgiveness of sins through repentance. The power of the resurrection resides in Christ. Christ is our rock upon whom we can build and not fall (see Hel. 5:12). "Blessed is the man that trusteth in the Lord, and whose hope the Lord is" (Jer. 17:7).

Building our lives upon our faith in the Savior Jesus Christ gives us hope—a perfect brightness of hope. We are filled with light and proceed to do good because of our hope. Hope is an attitude that can create a power and motivation to go forward. Nephi said, "Wherefore, ye must press forward with a steadfastness in Christ, having a perfect brightness of hope, and a love of God and of all men.

Wherefore, if ye shall press forward, feasting upon the word of Christ, and endure to the end, behold, thus saith the Father: Ye shall have eternal life" (2 Ne. 31:20).

Our lives, in order to have meaning and power to cope with adversity, must be riveted to hope. This is why it is an anchor for our souls. This is why we do good. Hope is not some word that simply means to have a positive attitude, it is rooted in Christ. It gives us the strength to go forward doing good works. We must seek hope through understanding the gospel plan. "Wherefore, whoso believeth in God might with surety hope for a better world, yea, even a place at the right hand of God, which hope cometh of faith, maketh an anchor to the souls of men, which would make them sure and stead-fast, always abounding in good works, being led to glorify God" (Ether 12:4).

As we repent we become meek and lowly and are blessed with the Spirit, and one of the blessings of the Spirit is hope.

"And the remission of sins bringeth meekness, and lowliness of heart; and because of meekness and lowliness of heart cometh the visitation of the Holy Ghost, which Comforter filleth with hope and perfect love, which love endureth by diligence unto prayer, until the end shall come, when all the saints shall dwell with God" (Moro. 8:26).

Our beloved prophet, Gordon B. Hinckley, has taught us that our message—the gospel message—is a message of hope for all mankind. He said, "Ours is truly a message of hope and reconciliation. It is a word of hope for all mankind, a beacon of eternal truth to which men may look as they lift their eyes and souls to their Creator and in the process come to recognize their common brotherhood" (*Teachings of Gordon B. Hinckley,* 373).

If hope is part of qualifying to serve, we must exert our effort in obtaining this hope—hope through and in the Lord Jesus Christ. Seek to understand and apply some of the following:

- Hope is centered in Jesus Christ. The opportunity to repent and gain eternal life is through our Savior who wrought the magnificent Atonement and Resurrection.
- Hope is connected to faith. The power of faith is increased with an attitude of hope.

- Hope gets things done. Hope, like faith, is a self-fulfilling prophecy, for it brings about the conditions to realize the vision that it sees for the future. Therefore, hope is an indispensable ally.
- Hope is a guide for life. Through the eyes of hope, you see opportunities that would otherwise be invisible—and therefore lost. Look at life from the perspective of hope.
- Count your blessings. In particular the blessings of the gospel and all those associated with eternal life. They will fill you with hope. Look at the bright and optimistic side of life. It's a choice you can make.
- Plan your agenda around hope. You can create a "feeling of hope" in life as you take the initiative to plan and carry out things that are enjoyable and uplifting.
- Be a problem solver. If you begin to feel dejected or hopeless, it becomes imperative to study the situation and make decisions to solve the problem. Think hope rather than feel despair.
- Work on long-range goals. Hope is a partner with action—the more you do the right kinds of things to attain your goals, the more hope you will have.
- Ask for hope. Look to God for help and comfort. The highest form of hope is one based on deep spiritual awakenings. Therefore, pray for hope each day.
- Be a leader of hope. A leader shares their vision of the future, and then helps generate the hope-filled actions that bring it about. Without hope, there is no leadership; with hope, leadership is empowered to lift and inspire.

It is our hope that makes the work of the Lord worthwhile. It is what sustains us in trials. It gives us purpose and direction in life. We are striving to be found worthy and to return to our Father in Heaven. This is what the Lord wants His missionaries to emulate.

Charity. Charity is the ultimate attribute of godliness that qualifies us for the work. It is obtaining the divine nature of Christ through faith, virtue, knowledge, temperance, patience, brotherly kindness, and godliness with all humility and diligence (see D&C 4:6). This pure love of Christ is total, complete, enduring and godlike. When we are possessed with this love our desires are like unto our Savior's—to bless and serve mankind. We have such compassion, love, and respect for others that we strive to serve them, not because we are *supposed* to, but because it is part of *who we are.*

Charity never fails. Christ did not fail His Father, nor did He fail us; His pure love motivated His great sacrifice—the eternal, infinite, vicarious Atonement. When we possess that love, we act in our lives according to the principles of the Atonement. When we possess this charity, we never fail. Through the Atonement of Christ, we begin to acquire this unconditional godly love, this divine nature of Christ. Can you see why this is what qualifies us for the work? We love God and His children so much, that we want nothing more than to serve them.

Charity is the goal for each of us as we seek to become like the Savior. We are nothing without Christ and we will be nothing without charity. The qualities of charity indicate the Christlike character that is involved in obtaining this magnificent virtue. We can see the joy that we will feel as we look at the qualities of charity. Surely this should be our goal. As Moroni teaches us, "And charity suffereth long, and is kind, and envieth not, and is not puffed up, seeketh not her own, is not easily provoked, thinketh no evil, and rejoiceth not in iniquity but rejoiceth in the truth, beareth all things, believeth all things, hopeth all things, endureth all things" (Moro. 7:45).

Why will it be well with us to have charity? Peter, that magnificent Apostle of the Lord, taught us that when we have charity we take upon ourselves the Savior's divine nature. By pursuing this path of righteousness our calling and election will be made sure (see 2 Pet. 1:3–12). As true followers of Christ, we seek to be like Him (see 3 Ne. 27:27), we keep the commandments and in all things seek to follow Christ and please our Heavenly Father. Then we will be made pure and be worthy of Their presence. We must seek after charity: "Wherefore, my beloved brethren, pray unto the Father with all the energy of heart, that ye may be filled with this love, which he hath bestowed upon all who are true followers of his Son, Jesus Christ; that ye may become the sons of God; that when he shall appear we shall be like him, for we shall see him as he is; that we may have this hope; that we may be purified even as he is pure" (Moro. 7:48).

President Benson has taught us concerning charity:

> The final and crowning virtue of the divine character is charity, or the pure love of Christ (see Moro. 7:47). If we would truly seek to be more like our Savior and Master, learning to love as He loves should be our highest goal. Mormon called charity "the greatest of all" (Moro. 7:46). . . . Charity never seeks selfish gratification. The pure love of Christ seeks only the eternal growth and joy of others.
>
> The Lord Jesus Christ liberated man from the world by the pure gospel of love. He demonstrated that man, through the love of God and through kindness and charity to His fellows, could achieve His highest potential. He lived the plain and sure doctrine of service, of doing good to all men—friends and enemies alike.
>
> (*The Teachings of Ezra Taft Benson*, 275.)

Here are just a few reminders to help us obtain charity.

- Pray with all our hearts to possess charity (see Moro. 7:48).
- Make a plan to increase our faith and follow the steps outlined in Doctrine and Covenants 4:6.
- Remember our Savior in all things (see D&C 20:77, 79).
- Create a new motto for our attitude and behavior. Do as Jesus would do (see 3 Ne. 27:27).
- Assist in the Lord's work with charity (see D&C 12:8).
- Clothe ourselves in all the qualities of charity (see D&C 88:125).

Christ's love for us endures forever. When we possess it, we have the capacity to bless others. Can we see the benefits and the blessings of charity exercised in our life? Let us with all the energy of our hearts, with all our souls, with all our minds, and in all of our decisions seek to be full of charity. Life will be beautiful and we will find peace as only the Lord can give (see D&C 19:23)—and we will be pure disciples of the Lord Jesus Christ (see John 13:34–35).

Let us remember the counsel from the prophet Mormon for his son Moroni: "And again, my beloved brethren, [a man] must needs have charity; for if he have not charity he is nothing; wherefore he must needs have charity" (Moro. 7:40–44).

An Eye Single to the Glory of God. Surely having an eye single to the glory of God makes our motives pure. And pure motives will qualify us to work for the Lord. Our motive is to build up His kingdom. Our motive is to bless lives. Our motive is to help people come unto Christ and partake of the goodness of God. It is not for self-aggrandizement, but it is to help people be happy. Our focus should be so strong that we have an overwhelming desire to help people be happy, keep the commandments, and be free from sin, even as was taught to the Whitmer brothers, Peter and John, when they asked the Prophet Joseph, "What is the most important thing we could do?" The answer was, "And now, behold, I say unto you, that the thing which will be of the most worth unto you will be to declare repentance unto this people, that you may bring souls unto me, that you may rest with them in the kingdom of my Father. Amen" (D&C 15:6). We can see that helping people come unto Christ is the most important thing. Why? Because we are focused on bringing ourselves and others to the Lord, which is His work. "For behold, this is my work and my glory—to bring to pass the immortality and eternal life of man" (Moses 1:39).

D&C 4:6—The Divine Nature of Christ.

"Remember faith, virtue, knowledge, temperance, patience, brotherly kindness, godliness, charity, humility, diligence" (D&C 4:6). Note the comparison to this in the Second Epistle of Peter 1:3–12. He includes most of the same virtues listed here in order that we might take on the divine nature of Christ. Are they important? They are the same qualities as those listed in Doctrine and Covenants 107:30 by which the presiding quorums of the Church are to make all unanimous decisions by. These are the qualities, along with faith, hope, and charity, that truly remind us of the things we need to do in order to serve with honor.

Attributes found in Doctrine and Covenants 4:6 are not given simply in random order. They provide a blueprint for personal character development and guidelines which will direct us back to our Father in Heaven. They are reiterated throughout the scriptures.

Faith. Notice how the Lord emphasizes again the principle of faith as part of the divine nature of Christ.

Virtue. This is the power within our lives, based on the righteousness that we possess.

Gospel knowledge. We must treasure up the words before we can teach the words. We will discuss this in depth later on.

Temperance and Patience. These are attributes that fall within charity; they are part of charity. Being calm and understanding with people is a way we can develop and show love for others. It is also an important expression of self-control.

Brotherly kindness. Compassion and caring for others is essential if we are to teach them the gospel.

Godliness. When we deny ourselves of all ungodliness—worldliness, selfishness, etc.—we will be more Christlike (see Moro. 7:48) and full of charity.

Humility. This is the beginning virtue of exaltation. It is knowing our relationship with God and depending upon Him. Then we obtain the fruits of humility—to be submissive, easily entreated, and teachable so that we can be instruments in the hands of the Lord Jesus Christ.

Diligence. This is work ethic. How diligent will we be? Will we give it our all? Will we work hard and smart? Will we do every needful thing to prepare, that we can be a pure disciple of Christ? Yes, these are the attributes that we must possess, this is the standard for the servants of the Lord.

So, now that we know we need the vision to succeed, how do we get it? Are we willing to prepare? So many people want to win, but as BYU Coach Lavell Edwards has often told his football teams, "Maybe they don't want to prepare to win." Preparation precedes the power to become a pure disciple of Christ. The following principles will help you prepare for this most important battle.

D&C 4:7—Ask, and Ye Shall Receive

We must never forget an eternal verity that requires us to ask (see James 1:5–6). Mighty prayer is part of being a disciple of Jesus Christ, which helps us to become a mighty instrument in His hands. Once we come to understand and appreciate these mighty words in section 4 we

gain a vision of the work and our role in bringing it about. Vision of
the work is revelation to your soul.

DESIRE

Now, if we have this vision and understand and appreciate it,
then we begin to have a desire. We want to be missionaries. We want
to share the gospel. We want to prepare. We want to be an instrument
in the hands of the Lord. This desire, when it swells within us, will
cause us to work harder. When Alma the Younger was converted, he
was like the sons of Mosiah; they couldn't wait to go on their
missions. When Enos was converted, he prayed all day and into the
night and his sins were forgiven, his guilt was swept away, and he was
truly converted. He began to pray for the Nephites, and he prayed for
the Lamanites, and then he implored Heavenly Father to save the
record, because he wanted everyone to hear the record because it was
so good and so precious. You see what happens? Our desire begins to
increase when our conversion to Christ is real. We *want* to be
missionaries for the Lord. When we have a clear vision, we have a
desire, and then we become worthy disciples of Jesus Christ.

A WORTHY INSTRUMENT

Earlier in my life I was a practicing dentist. I would go to the
hospital and do oral surgery to remove the third molars (wisdom teeth).
I can still remember preparing for surgery with the nurses around, the
anesthesiologists in the operating room, and everything ready to go for
the operation. Then I would say, "scalpel," and the scalpel was in my
hand. I would retract the cheek a little bit and make an incision, lay
back the tissue, and then I would start to remove the impacted third
molar. Those instruments did whatever I wanted them to do because I
had them in my hand and I was in control. I knew what I was
supposed to do and so I was hopefully very kind and efficient. Well,
you know what? That experience is an analogy for missionary work.
The instruments were clean, pure, and sharp. Thus, each instrument
could meet its intended purpose in my hand, for I was the doctor and I
was in charge. And that's what our relationship is with our Savior. He is
our master, and we are instruments in His hands—submissive to His
will, provided we are clean and pure and know our purpose. As we

come to better understand missionary work and the need for this marvelous gospel to be spread, we will want nothing more than to be worthy servants of our Savior—before, during, and after our missions.

OBEDIENT DISCIPLES

In the mission field there's a great law—it's called obedience. In our mission, when I was president, it was called immediate, exact, and courageous obedience. Obedience is built upon love, faith, and trust in God. When we live the principle of obedience, we will be more diligent in being immediately, exactly, and courageously obedient.

I know a story of a young boy who wanted to fly a kite. He and his father purchased a kite along with two spools of string, which they put on one big spool. They fixed it all up and went out to fly their kite. The kite started taking off. "Dad, look at it go, look at it go!" the boy cried. Soon the kite soared higher and higher. They let all the string out. The boy pulled the string and said, "Dad, the string is holding it down. Look how tight it is. It's really tight. Let's cut it so the kite can fly up higher."

The dad said, "No, you don't understand, son. This is what holds the kite up. It needs the string."

The boy said, "Dad, look!" and he pulled on the string. "See, it's holding, it's tight, it's holding it down."

The dad answered, "No son, the string helps the kite fly."

"No it doesn't," insisted the boy.

"So you want to cut the string?" asked the dad.

"Yes, I want to let it fly up all the way, all the way to the clouds," replied the boy.

The dad said, "okay," and he took out his pocketknife and let the boy cut the string. Well, you know what happened next, the kite came crashing down to the ground.

The boy looked at his dad and asked, "Why didn't it go higher?"

The father replied, "Son, the string was part of the law by which the kite could fly." This boy learned a lesson about following temporal laws that day. And, as with physical laws, everything spiritual is based upon a law. "There is a law, irrevocably decreed in heaven before the foundations of this world, upon which all blessings are predicated—And when we obtain any blessing from God, it is by obedience to that law upon which it is predicated" (D&C 130: 20–21). I imagine that boy was grateful for the string the next time he flew a kite. When we understand the purpose of commandments, we want to keep them. We get the blessing upon which the law is based. If we eat properly, we feel good. If we study, we learn.

Now, do you know what we get when we're obedient? When we're obedient we receive the greatest gift in all the world—the gift of the Spirit. Every Sunday we go to church and partake of the sacrament, and at the end of the sacramental prayer it says, "and keep his commandments which he hath given [us]," (or in other words, if we are obedient) "that [we] may always have his Spirit to be with [us]." The Spirit will guide us, it will testify for us, it will lead us, it will correct us, it will comfort us, and it will show us all things that we should do (see 2 Ne. 32:5). We cannot do anything in the mission field without having the Spirit, and we can't have the Spirit unless we choose to be obedient. This is the hardest thing for missionaries to understand. If we are exactly, immediately, and courageously obedient in all things, the Lord will bless us. This life is a test to see if we will obey (see Abr. 3:25). When obedience becomes our quest we will be happy and we will grow. Our desire to serve God and His children increases our desire to be obedient. Our obedience increases our desire to serve. This is why obedience brings such happiness in our lives.

LIVING BY THE SPIRIT

When we become obedient we become Spirit directed in all things, which is something we all desire as we come to understand our mission. We will be led by the Spirit, not knowing beforehand the things we should do (see 1 Ne. 4:6). We can have the Spirit all day long and every day. The question is, will we become worthy to have it? When we desire to do good, we feel the Spirit. We will want to search the scriptures, say our prayers, and be kind to our fellowmen. The Spirit will show us and help us do all the things we should do. Sometimes we feel, "I'm not ready, I don't know how to do this, how can I ever do it?" The Lord and the Spirit will assist us. "I will go before your face. I will be on your right hand and on your left, and my Spirit shall be in your hearts, and mine angels round about you, to bear you up" (D&C 84:88). The Lord is there helping every missionary, and everyone who strives to live by the power of the Spirit. We give the credit to the Lord for all things. Become an instrument for the Lord and a conduit for the Spirit.

WORK

When we become Spirit directed in all things, we will be willing to work with faith, diligence and patience.

To prepare to be missionaries, we need to know how to work. Think of how good you feel when you work hard for something and accomplish it. Now imagine how much more amazing it would be to spend your time doing the most important work—spreading the gospel. When I was a mission president, I observed that missionaries who had taken extra time and effort to do well in school or jobs knew how to work; they were always that much better as missionaries. They were successful. Others, I had to teach how to work. I would have to tell them the story about how I was raised on a farm, and how, on our farm, we had to work or we got spanked. I learned right off that we worked or we perished. You don't want to spiritually or emotionally perish in the mission field.

President Benson has taught us that:

> One of the greatest secrets of missionary work, is *work*. If a missionary works he will get the Spirit; if he gets the Spirit, he will teach by the Spirit; and if he teaches by the Spirit, he will touch the hearts of the people, and he will be happy. Then there will be no homesickness nor worrying about families, for all time and talents and interests are centered on the work of the ministry. Work, work, work—there is no satisfactory substitute, especially in missionary work.
>
> (Ezra Taft Benson, *Come Unto Christ*
> [Salt Lake City: Deseret Book, 1983], 95.)

In the mission field, all the missionaries knew that President Pinegar loved them, but if they didn't want to work, I was very sad and I would call them in and say, "I don't feel so good. I don't know if you're working as hard as the Lord would want you to work." We would discuss the Atonement. Their gratitude would increase and they would start to cry, then I'd start to cry, and we'd cry together, and we'd agree that we would work harder, because there is nothing more joyous than working for the Lord. Think what the Savior and all the prophets have done for us. Appreciate what they did. Can you imagine what they went through? The price is high, but it's worth it. Remember, learn to work. To prepare, get a job and organize your time wisely.

CONCLUSION

Missionaries who are prepared with every needful thing will reap the blessings of the Lord in all things. When they have a hard day, they get up and do it again, and they never quit, they never give up, they never give in, they never give out. They are always just working, doing the Lord's work. This is what it is to serve with all our heart, might, mind, and strength. This is the person we all desire to become.

My dear friends, this is the gospel. This is what we can become. We can be the missionaries we envision. We can be worthy, obedient, diligent servants who live by the Spirit. It only depends on how willing we are to become so. The gospel is glorious and so many are waiting for it, aching for it. The field is white. It is now our opportunity to qualify ourselves to harvest it.

CHAPTER 3
RAISING THE BAR—THE LORD'S EXPECTATION

President Hinckley recently said, "The time has come when we must raise the standards of those who are called to serve as ambassadors of the Lord Jesus Christ to the world" ("Missionary Service," *First Worldwide Leadership Training Meeting*, Jan. 2003, 17).

In today's world, the Lord needs the greatest missionaries that have ever served. They must be worthy and prepared. The Lord needs more virtuous, righteous, free-from-sin disciples—worthy in every way. He needs missionaries who are more faithful, obedient, honest, hard-working and doing the will of the Lord. He needs more doctrinally sound and testimony-bearing missionaries who are full of faith, hope, and charity; missionaries who have lived faith unto repentance; missionaries who preach the word of God by the Spirit, that people may come unto Christ; missionaries with the attributes and skills necessary to serve with all their heart, might, mind, and strength.

Elder Ballard, in his magnificent sermon in general conference entitled "The Greatest Generation of Missionaries," said:

> What we need now is the greatest generation of missionaries in the history of the Church. We need worthy, qualified, spiritually energized missionaries who, like Helaman's 2,000 stripling warriors, are "exceedingly valiant for courage and also for strength and activity" and who are "true at all times in whatsoever thing they [are] entrusted" (Alma 53:20).

As an Apostle of the Lord Jesus Christ, I call upon you to begin right now—tonight—to be fully and completely worthy. Resolve and commit to yourselves and to God that from this moment forward you will strive diligently to keep your hearts, hands, and minds pure and unsullied from any kind of moral transgression. Resolve to avoid pornography as you would avoid the most insidious disease, for that is precisely what it is. Resolve to completely abstain from tobacco, alcohol, and illegal drugs. Resolve to be honest. Resolve to be good citizens and to abide by the laws of the land in which you live. Resolve that from this night forward you will never defile your body or use language that is vulgar and unbecoming to a bearer of the priesthood.

And that is not all we expect of you, my young brethren. We expect you to have an understanding and a solid testimony of the restored gospel of Jesus Christ. We expect you to work hard. We expect you to be covenant makers and covenant keepers. We expect you to be missionaries to match our glorious message.

Now these are high standards. We understand that, but we do not apologize for them. They reflect the Lord's standards for you to receive the Melchizedek Priesthood, to enter the temple, to serve as missionaries, and to be righteous husbands and fathers. There's nothing new in them, nothing you haven't heard before. But tonight we call upon you, our young brethren of the Aaronic priesthood, to rise up, to measure up, and to be fully prepared to serve the Lord.

(*Ensign*, Nov. 2002, 47.)

We can see that the requirements have been raised. We must rise to this expectation. When we understand and appreciate doctrines, principles, concepts, and covenants of the gospel, our attitudes and behavior will change. We will be the kind of missionary the Lord expects us to be.

THE BAR HAS BEEN RAISED

President Hinckley has said, "We simply cannot permit those who have not qualified themselves as to worthiness to go into the world to speak the glad tidings of the gospel" (*First Worldwide Leadership Training Meeting,* Jan. 2003, 17).

We now understand from the First Presidency's statement on missionary work that there are transgressions that will disqualify young men and women from missionary service (see "Statement on Missionary Work from the First Presidency and the Quorum of the Twelve Apostles," 11 Dec. 2002). The Lord indeed expects us to qualify in order to serve. It is a privilege, not a right.

Worthiness and Preparedness

Elder Ballard taught us that if we are not on track, if we are not doing what is right, we must put ourselves on track. We must put ourselves in a situation where we can become worthy. He said:

> Many of you are already on this track, and we commend you for your worthiness and determination. For those of you who are not, let tonight be the beginning of your preparation process. If you find yourself wanting in worthiness, resolve to make the appropriate changes—beginning right now. If you think you need to talk to your father and your bishop about any sins you may have committed, don't wait; do it now. They will help you to repent and change so you can take your place as a member of the greatest generation of missionaries.
>
> ("The Greatest Generation of Missionaries" *Ensign,* Nov. 2002, 47–48.)

Don't wait to repent. Be prepared. We must reiterate that the bar has been raised. We cannot knowingly do wrong and then say, "Oh, I'll repent before my mission and then go." Elder Ballard emphasized this point in October 2002:

> Please understand this: the bar that is the standard for missionary service is being raised. The day of the "repent and go" missionary is over. You know what I'm talking about, don't you, my young brothers? Some young men have the mistaken idea that they can be involved in sinful behavior and then repent when they're [almost 19] so they can go on their mission at 19. While it is true that you can repent of sins, you may or

you may not qualify to serve. It is far better to keep yourselves clean and pure and valiant . . .

("The Greatest Generation of Missionaries," *Ensign*, Nov. 2002, 48.)

Elders and sisters, there are consequences for sin. Sometimes, we think that when we repent, it's a single moment, an event. It is not an event. Repentance is a process. If you were to fall off a cliff, break your leg, and get a compound fracture, and then say, "Oh, I wish I hadn't done that," your leg wouldn't be healed instantly. It requires a process. It takes time. Certain things have to be done for that bone to heal. The same principle applies in preparing for a mission. Sometimes people think that if they confess and say they won't do it again, that the consequences of sin are over. They are not over. The spirit, heart, and mind often take time to heal from the consequences of sin. Let me reiterate—it is not an event. It is a process, and it will take time.

Because we don't always recognize that there are consequences of sin, many people mistakenly think they can go on a mission, no matter what they've done, if they just confess. Some will now be withheld from service because their sins are so grievous. This does not preclude them from being exalted or from being married in the temple. It merely means that at this time in their life the consequences of sin are very severe. In preparing to serve, Elder Ballard has suggested some things prospective missionaries should be doing:

- Developing a meaningful prayer relationship with your Heavenly Father.
- Keeping the Sabbath day holy.
- Working and putting part of your earnings in a savings account.
- Paying a full and honest tithing.
- Limiting the amount of time spent playing computer games. How many kills you can make in a minute with a computer game will have zero effect on your capacity to be a good missionary.
- Giving the Lord more of your time by studying the scriptures and gaining an understanding of the marvelous message of the Restoration that we have for the world.
- Serving others and sharing your testimony with them.

("The Greatest Generation of Missionaries," *Ensign*, Nov. 2002, 48.)

Parents, priesthood leaders, and various other friends and family should help missionaries be prepared. Brothers and sisters, seek the advice of your parents. Go to seminary. Take your missionary preparation courses at your institute or Church university. Do every needful thing. Read books on missionary work. Search the scriptures on missionary work. There are things you can do individually and things you can do as a family to help prepare. There are things you can do in your priesthood and Young Women classes, and in preparation courses held by your stake.

The most important thing is that we must prepare earlier and better. We must devote time to preparation. Being prepared as a missionary is not having a new suit or a new wardrobe or new scriptures. Being prepared as a missionary is a changing of heart, of mind, of soul. It is the very essence of becoming a disciple of Jesus Christ.

Prophets have upheld this standard from the beginning of the missionary program.

Brigham Young states the following:

> If the Elders cannot go with clean hands and pure hearts, they had better stay here. Do not go thinking, when you arrive at the Missouri River, at the Mississippi, at the Ohio, or at the Atlantic, that then you will purify yourselves; but start from here with clean hands and pure hearts, and be pure from the crown of the head to the soles of your feet; then live so every hour. Go in that manner, and in that manner labor, and return again as clean as a piece of pure white paper. This is the way to go; and if you do not do that, your hearts will ache.
>
> (*Brigham Young, Discourses of Brigham Young,*
> sel. John A. Widtsoe [Salt Lake City: Deseret Book, 1954], 323.)

President Woodruff also noted:

> All the messengers in the vineyard should be righteous and holy men and call upon the Lord in mighty prayer, in order to prevail. It is the privilege of every Elder in Israel, who is laboring in the vineyard, if he will live up to his privileges, to have dreams, visions and revelations, and the Holy Ghost as a constant companion, that he may be able thoroughly to gather out the

blood of Israel and the meek of the earth, and bring them into
the fold of Christ.

(Wilford Woodruff, *The Discourses of Wilford Woodruff,*
ed. G. Homer Durham [Salt Lake City: Bookcraft, 1969], 101.)

THE DEMANDS OF MISSIONARY WORK

Worthiness must be our main focus in preparation, but it is not the
only factor to consider. Physical well-being can also play a prominent
role in preparing for a mission. The Brethren have recently explained:
"Those individuals not able to meet the physical, mental, and emotional
demands of full-time missionary work are honorably excused. . . . They
may be called to serve in other rewarding capacities" ("Statement on
Missionary Work from the First Presidency and the Quorum of the
Twelve Apostles," 11 Dec. 2002). We must be physically healthy. We
must be able to endure the rigors of missionary work. It is not easy.
Sometimes we are so enthused we think we can do anything, but if you
had an injured leg and were asked to run the 100-yard dash, it might
not be possible to win the race. You want to win, you've done as much
as you can to win, but you simply can't run fast enough because of your
situation.

It is the same thing in missionary work. If you have serious physical
limitations and you cannot stand the rigors of full-time serivce, it is not
required of you to serve a full-time mission. Mosiah 4:27 states "it is
not requisite that a man should run faster than he has strength." The
Lord does not expect us to do things that we cannot do. This does not
mean that we are unworthy. The Lord loves us. Remember this: earth is
our mission. *Everything* on this earth is a mission from the day we are
born until the day we die; we are always missionaries for the Lord Jesus
Christ. We are His disciples. We can help people come unto Christ by
befriending our neighbors, friends, and classmates. Everyone knows
someone who is not a member of our Church. Help that person come
to know that Jesus is the Christ. Befriend them. Teach them. Nurture
them. Invite the missionaries to see them.

Because we're not full-time proselyting missionaries does not mean
that we can't be missionaries for the Lord Jesus Christ. So if physical
conditions prevent you from serving, you are honorably excused, and
there should be no guilt. You can even serve Church-service missions

right from home. It's a joy. I'm a Church-service missionary. I get to go teach at the Senior MTC every week. It is truly a privilege! Everyone can be a missionary every day. If physical requirements prevent you from going, be of good cheer. Heavenly Father loves you. You are his son or his daughter. You can serve in whatever way you are able while you're still at home.

Some of us struggle with emotional problems—a chemical imbalance, or whatever it might be. There are certain mental stresses that can cause panic attacks or anxiousness. These emotional stresses can affect our physical bodies in very severe ways and can prevent us from serving the Lord on a full-time mission. Unless the condition is stabilized with proper medication, the Lord and the prophet have excused us from the work. Again, these challenges have no effect on our personal worthiness or desire to serve.

If we have any physical or emotional difficulties that might prevent our full-time service, do not overburden the bishop by saying, "The Lord loves me. He will make me well," or "I have enough faith that I'll be okay." If you qualify medically and your condition is stabilized and cleared through a doctor, then you can serve full-time. But don't put guilt upon yourself. Don't beat yourself up because you're not emotionally or physically able to participate in the strains of full-time missionary service. Let the Lord guide your life and trust in His wisdom for you.

Regardless of whether we serve full-time missions, service missions, or just everyday missions, one of the great needs in today's missionary effort is more and better prepared missionaries. President Spencer W. Kimball has said:

> I am asking that we start earlier and train our missionaries better in every branch and every ward in the world. . . . I am asking for missionaries who have been carefully indoctrinated and trained through the family and the organizations of the Church, and who come to the mission with a great desire. I am asking . . . that we train prospective missionaries much better, much earlier, much longer, so that each anticipates his mission with great joy.
>
> ("When the World Will Be Converted," *Ensign*, Oct. 1974, 7.)

BEING BEYOND REPROACH

One of the best things about serving as a missionary, and preparing to serve as one, is the frequent opportunity to evaluate yourself and see if you are "beyond reproach"—innocent and pure. Personal evaluations of our lives have a way of showing our positive qualities as well as some slightly negative tendencies we might have.

To continually evaluate yourself—beginning now—you start with your head and check to see if it is "on straight," as the saying goes. Is your mind programmed to keep you moving along the straight and narrow? Is your mind in control of your life, your choices, your reactions, your actions? Or are you controlled by emotions—easy to anger, easy to self-pity, easy to have hurt feelings, quick to be jealous or resentful of another's success?

Every missionary is set apart so that he or she may be enhanced by the Spirit of God, that is, be even better at this work than he or she might naturally be. Think of the words Paul the Apostle wrote to Timothy, whom he considered his dearly beloved son: "Wherefore I put thee in remembrance that thou stir up the gift of God, which is in thee by the putting on of my hands. For God hath not given us the spirit of fear; but of power, and of love, and of a sound mind" (2 Tim. 1:6–7).

Now, as part of this important self-evaluation, move to your heart. Look deep inside. What do you see? Consider the questions listed in Alma 5 in terms of your own life and feelings.

> And now behold, I ask of you, my brethren of the church, have ye spiritually been born of God? Have ye received his image in your countenances? Have ye experienced this mighty change in your hearts?
>
> Do ye exercise faith in the redemption of him who created you? Do you look forward with an eye of faith, and view this mortal body raised in immortality, and this corruption raised in incorruption, to stand before God to be judged according to the deeds which have been done in the mortal body?
>
> (Alma 5:14–15.)

These revealing verses are but a fraction of the insights that come to people who read Alma and match themselves against the high standards presented in that chapter.

We are happy when we are "beyond reproach." We enjoy success. We wax confident before God and feel His approbation. We think of others before ourselves and virtue garnishes our thoughts.

You can meet the challenge. You can be a pure disciple of Jesus Christ. You can be worthy, prepared, and a clean instrument in the hands of the Lord. You can make a difference in the lives of your brothers and sisters. You can help them taste of the joy that you have. You can do all that the Lord expects you to do as you turn your will over to the Lord.

CONCLUSION

The bar has been raised. We, as future missionaries, and especially full-time proselyting missionaries, have been instructed by living prophets. We should prepare to be disciples of Jesus Christ by doing every needful thing, as well as assessing our social, emotional, intellectual, and physical health—doing our best to be as healthy as possible and leaving the rest to the Lord. Above all, we must become spiritually strong.

Your spiritual strength is so essential in serving. If, within your heart, you do not have this spirit of undying commitment to the covenant that you've made with the Lord, there will be days when you will not be able to serve as well as you should, both on and off your mission. We need spiritual strength in order to be the kind of missionaries we should be. There are souls to be saved. There are souls to be strengthened. There are souls to be rescued. There are families to be activated. There is work to be done. Wherever we are, this is part of our duty, our obligation, our calling as members of the Church and kingdom of God, disciples of the Lord Jesus Christ. Surely we can all serve in the ways that the Lord will provide for us to serve, whether as full-time missionaries, Church-service missionaries, or even as members fulfilling our Church callings. We can all serve our God and our fellowmen by helping them come unto Christ and enjoy the blessings of exaltation.

We must become missionaries to match the message, disciples of Jesus Christ, not just for a full-time mission, but for life. We need to be full of faith. We need to be moved to repentance. We must have a desire to serve. We must be living worthy of a temple recommend—we must maintain the worthiness that is expected of us in order to serve.

CHAPTER 4
BECOMING PURE DISCIPLES OF THE LORD JESUS CHRIST

Discipleship is a sacred trust given to each of us because we are followers of Christ. We are willing to stand as witnesses of God at all times and in all things and in all places (see Mosiah 18:8–9) because we are His disciples, His witnesses, His servants, and His friends.

As we reflect on our sacred calling, we must consider our effect on others. Does our demeanor radiate love? Do we inspire trust? Are we always exemplary in our behavior? Do we appear light-minded? Is our conversation focused on the work or things of the world? Let's make the decision to *always* be a "light," to *always* live up to the standard of the gospel, and to *always* do as Jesus would do.

AMBASSADORS OF CHRIST

As missionaries and missionary leaders we talk of Christ, we preach of Christ, we testify of Christ. All of us who are serving the Lord in or out of the mission field are His disciples and ambassadors. We must make ourselves worthy to be called such. The light that we hold (see 3 Ne. 18:24) is the Lord Jesus Christ. As Elder Hans B. Ringger so eloquently explains:

> The foundation and guiding light for all our decisions is the gospel of Jesus Christ and His message to the world. The teachings of Christ must be embedded in our desire to choose the right and in our wish to find happiness. His righteous life must be reflected in our own actions. The Lord not only teaches love, He *is* love. He not only preached the importance of faith, repentance, baptism,

and the gift of the Holy Ghost, He *lived* accordingly. His life reflected the gospel that He preached. There was and is total harmony between His thoughts and His actions.

("Choose You This Day," *Ensign,* May 1990, 25.)

We cannot bear testimony of His Church and His kingdom without knowing Jesus Christ, the Savior of the world. When we know Christ, we can hold up His light; He is the light and the life of the world (see John 8:12). And when we hold up that light, then we truly become His disciples.

In 3 Nephi, Jesus Christ tells His disciples that they are "the light of this people," (3 Ne. 12:14) and He explains that they will bless all of Heavenly Father's children. Christ also instructed the Nephites not to put their light under a bushel, but to put it "on a candlestick, and it giveth light to all that are in the house" (3 Ne. 12:15). That same instruction applies to each of us; when we possess the light of Jesus Christ, we must not put it under a bushel. That light must be held up, and then—and only then—will we be true and worthy representatives of our Savior, Jesus Christ.

President Gordon B. Hinckley observed that we represent Christ's army:

> In this work there must be commitment. There must be devotion. We are engaged in a great eternal struggle that concerns the very souls of the sons and daughters of God. We are not losing. We are winning. We will continue to win if we will be faithful and true. We *can* do it. We *must* do it. We *will* do it. There is nothing the Lord has asked of us that in faith we cannot accomplish.
>
> ("The War We Are Winning," *Ensign,* Nov. 1986, 44.)

We are charged to be His soldiers, to find and help save our brothers and sisters. Each one of us needs help. Sister Pinegar is my keeper, and she works hard to help me do what's right. I pray that each of you will seek to be shepherds like Christ, to be your brothers' and sisters' keeper, and as you work to help each other, remember: "Inasmuch as ye have done it unto one of the least of these my brethren, ye have done it unto me" (Matt. 25:40).

We must not be manipulative salespeople. We must be disciples of Christ. All the knowledge and skills we learn must be magnified by the power of God, by the attributes of Christ, by the Spirit of the Lord, by the mind and will of the Lord.

EVALUATING OUR LIVES AND BECOMING LIKE CHRIST

As discussed in the last chapter, we must constantly evaluate where we stand in the gospel. Consider the following:

1. Are you focusing your life in the world on Christ as the Savior of mankind and the one whom you serve? How much do you appreciate the Savior and His atoning sacrifice and your desire to be like Him?
2. Is your desire increasing to bless the lives of others and to lose yourself in their service?
3. Is your testimony of the Book of Mormon and the Prophet Joseph Smith increasing?
4. Are your prayers changing?
5. Is your love and testimony of the scriptures, particularly the Book of Mormon, increasing?

We grow and become like Christ through recognizing where we are, and what we need to do to become more like Him. Once we evaluate our lives, we set goals and make plans to keep the commandments and the covenants we have made. Unfortunately, some of us never recognize where we are because we never take the time to evaluate our lives. Every day should be an evaluating day, a goal-setting day, a plan-making day, and a living day.

Alma 5 is the great evaluation chapter—a great example of the questions we can ask ourselves as we're evaluating our own lives. In Alma 5, Alma the Younger asks the people to consider at least forty-three questions about their spiritual progress. Can you imagine the scene?

Alma was speaking by way of commandment to Church members, reminding them of the goodness of God in their lives. He asked the people (and I'm paraphrasing), "Has a remembrance of the captivity of your fathers brought you to remember the mercy and long-suffering of God towards you? Do you realize He delivered your soul from hell?"

Alma continues, speaking about their ancestors and how God "changed their hearts; yea, he awakened them out of a deep sleep, and they awoke unto God. Behold, they were in the midst of darkness; nevertheless, their souls were illuminated by the light of the everlasting word" (v. 7). Our souls, too, are illuminated by the everlasting word.

"Yea," Alma continues, "they were encircled about by the bands of death, and the chains of hell, and an everlasting destruction did await them" (v. 7).

And then Alma talks about experiencing a mighty change of heart, and asks those in the congregation if they had been spiritually born of God (see v. 14).

Can you imagine that? He's talking to Church members (like us), asking if they realize that it's not enough to just be baptized and receive the Holy Ghost; he's saying that we must be spiritually born of God.

In verse 13 Alma observes: "And behold, [Alma the Elder] preached the word unto your fathers, and a mighty change was also wrought in their hearts, and they humbled themselves and put their trust in the true and living God. And behold, they were faithful until the end; therefore they were saved." Notice how it is humility, being meek and lowly, that creates a place for the word in our hearts, and the word then brings a willingness to change.

There are more treasures in Alma 5. Through the Spirit and revelation, Alma asks the people if they've been stripped of envy and pride. He asks them who mocks or persecutes others. Listen to the fate of someone who belittles another one of Heavenly Father's children: "Wo unto such an one, for he is not prepared, and the time is at hand that he must repent or he cannot be saved!" (v. 31).

Alma pleads with all of his heart, and I plead with all of my heart, that we all might listen to the words of Christ and examine ourselves as suggested in Alma 5.

Like Alma, I also speak to you, the disciples of Christ. We must honestly look at ourselves and evaluate our lives and actions. Each day we can say, "I am a divine child of God, and I can be better each day, a step at a time." Don't overwhelm yourself; but whether you're nineteen or ninety-nine, each day strive to be better than you were the day before.

Oh, you missionaries and missionaries-to-be are so good! You'll increase in your faith because you'll have a vision of who you are.

You'll possess the pure love of Christ because you know who you are. You'll choose to be exactly obedient because you love your God.

Each day I pray that you'll take a moment to look in the mirror and evaluate your life. Then, go and do as Jesus would do. Every day, let us be as the Savior, Jesus Christ, would have us be. And what manner of men and women ought we to be? (see 3 Ne. 27:27). The Savior tells us: "Therefore I would that ye should be perfect even as I, or your Father who is in heaven is perfect" (3 Ne. 12:48). That leaves room for improvement in anyone's life.

BECOMING A DISCIPLE OF CHRIST: A MIGHTY CHANGE AND A PURE HEART

Since we are considering doing something about our lives, our personal being, our body and our spirit in order to bring ourselves into a compatible state with the Savior, we should consider the elements of change. What is involved?

Six Principles to Effect Change

First, we must have respect for Heavenly Father and our leaders. They teach us, they counsel us, they set the standard. They are our leaders and exemplars.

Second, we need to be awakened to the reason for change—a need to be like Christ! "Need" indicates a stronger attitude than "want." For eternal goals we surely should move from a state of "wanting" to be Christlike and to qualify for dwelling in His presence towards a thrust of, "I will go and do the things which the Lord hath commanded" (1 Ne. 3:7).

Third, we must look inward upon the secret heart and the spiritual core, upon the essence of intelligence that has always been, and discern our relationship to Christ and what the mission we've come to perform is. "Of what worth is my soul?" the thoughtful person could ask. And the question finds answer in our awareness of our precious value to God. We are the divine children of God the Eternal Father. This knowledge naturally creates motivation to fulfill our potential.

Fourth, a person must take action to move from vague generalities to specific goals. It is information to be acted upon. One moves from a vague and delaying type of behavior to the purposeful and healing act of full repentance. Stop doing what you shouldn't be doing at once! Or start doing those things that should be done at once! Understanding of old principles and new information can be motivating, but setting a definite goal is valuable for real success. For example, one might say, "I want to make it to the celestial kingdom." That is a generality. But to say, "I am going to pay a full tithe this month and every month," is a specific goal that can easily become a reality. The Savior teaches line upon line because that is most effective—it is the same with our personal accomplishments. With small, measurable goals, life isn't as overwhelming.

Fifth, establish a system of values to operate within. It has been said that where your treasure is, there your heart is also (see Matt. 6:21). And what the heart is concerned with, the mind follows. Action trails soon after. It seems obvious that to set the heart upon eternal values protects one against wallowing in earthbound pleasures only. So, we look to the feelings of the heart for any effort to change; we put our value upon the things of Christ if we would be like Christ.

Sixth, commit to Christ. One has to make up one's mind that Christ lives and is our leader. We will stand by Him "no matter what," and even "no matter who." We must be determined to take the course of action necessary to bring the needed goal and its eternal rewards. We might say our life depends upon it—eternal life, in this case!

The total process of change is a continuing one. It is bound with the first principles and all the ordinances of the full gospel of Jesus Christ: faith in Jesus Christ, the man and His mission, His role and His authority as the Son of God; repentance, or turning around from anything anti-Christ in our life and beginning the move in a direction that will take us back into His presence; submitting humbly to the immersion of our whole bodies in the waters of baptism that we might bury our sins therein and emerge clean every whit to accept the gift of the Holy Ghost by the laying on of hands. And from there we begin our true growth in understanding principles with eternal overtones, and applying them to every aspect of our life—problem and pleasure, challenge and reward!

This is where the continuum exists. We do not understand all things at once. We grow and are given understanding from God of all things, a little at a time as we are ready to receive them—line upon line, grace upon grace (see 2 Ne. 28:30).

So, change is ever with us, whether we like it or not. And if we don't move forward in change, we will move backward. The opposite of progression is retrogression. Ours is the task to move steadily in the direction of perfection. If we slip a step, we must repent and give thanks for the Atonement of Christ, then right our wrong, and start upward on the path to exaltation once more. What enlightenment comes when one really awakens to the strength and power of His Spirit! For the spirit can direct the body. It can be a strong, sweet, lovely director of the body's actions. Or it can be uncultivated in the ways of God and be weak, disobedient, bitter, and finally, hateful. Exaltation later, and even joy in this life, does not result from such lack of discipline.

Our spirits are truly affected by our environment to such a point that we mirror it. We behave as we are taught by example, pressure, or principle, unless some other force stronger than environment comes into play in our lives and masters our souls in a more righteous and enlightened manner. The spirit relinquishes its chance to obey the Father if it chooses the harrowing trail of the world. This is in keeping with the early, premortal battle between the coercive approach of the adversary and the Savior's gentle, wise approach to the salvation of man through the protection of their agency.

The interesting thing to remember, though, is that superior guidance for self-improvement must come at a person's level of faith and be continually nourished at their rate of absorption. You can, as we recall the truth of the old adage, drive a horse to water, but you cannot make it drink. When the word of the Lord comes into a life, as compared to Alma's seed in Alma 32:27, it will not be received unless people are in a "state of preparedness" to receive it. In Matthew 3 we see the comparison fully made in the parable of the sower, which vividly and appropriately describes the many threats to the flourishing of the seed. Before people will change—or can change—they must have hearts ready to receive the word—the seed of truth. Then, the nourishing can insure a fruitful yield in life.

Love is interwoven into all six principles to effect change: (1) respect is a form of love; (2) people need love more than anything else and love is the strongest motivation; (3) self-esteem, in a sense, is love of self in its proper setting; (4) love is a verb and is expressed with specific acts of service; (5) you value what you love, and likewise love what you value; (6) acts of commitment, born of love, are many (see John 3:16, 14:15).

As a set-apart missionary, you are a disciple of Jesus Christ. Elder Bruce R. McConkie has said of this commission:

> I am called of God. My authority is above that of the kings of the earth. By revelation I have been selected as a personal representative of the Lord Jesus Christ. He is my Master and He has chosen me to represent Him. To stand in His place, to say and do what He himself would say and do if He personally were ministering to the very people to whom He has sent me. My voice is His voice, and my acts are His acts; my words are His words and my doctrine is His doctrine. My commission is to do what He wants done. To say what He wants said. To be a living modern witness in word and deed of the divinity of His great and marvelous latter-day work.
>
> ("How Great Is My Calling" [address delivered while serving as president of the Australian Mission, 1961–64].)

The Power of the Holy Ghost

If I would pray for anything for the missionaries scattered all over the world, I would pray that the Spirit of the Lord would come upon them with such power that they would never want to do anything wrong again. When we're filled with the power of the Holy Ghost, we simply cannot sin. That's why the Nephite nation, in 3 Nephi 19:9, prayed "for that which they most desired; and they desired that the Holy Ghost should be given unto them."

Why would the Nephites desire the Holy Ghost so fervently? Elder Parley P. Pratt answered this question when he described the extraordinary characteristics of this remarkable power:

> The gift of the Holy Spirit . . . quickens all the intellectual faculties, increases, enlarges, expands and purifies all the natural passions and affections; and adapts them, by the gift of wisdom, to their lawful use. It inspires . . . virtue, kindness, goodness, tenderness, gentleness and charity. It develops beauty of person, form and features. It tends to health, vigor, animation, and social feeling. It develops and

invigorates all the faculties of the physical and intellectual man. It strengthens, invigorates, and gives tone to the nerves. In short, it is, as it were, marrow to the bone, joy to the heart, light to the eyes, music to the ears, and life to the whole being.

(Parley P. Pratt, *Key to the Science of Theology: Voice of Warning* [Salt Lake City: Deseret Book, 1965], 101.)

All you need for a strong testimony is the companionship of the Holy Ghost. Just because you can't move a mountain yet, don't ever think your testimony isn't strong, because it is. Every testimony that's born is not born of man, but born of God by the power of the Holy Ghost. When we bear testimony, it's not you or me; it's the Spirit of God, and that's powerful.

Just the other day I got a letter. "Dear President Pinegar," it began, "We didn't know what we were doing. We didn't know which way was up, but we took ten copies of the Book of Mormon, we placed ten copies, and we have nine referrals. Is that pretty good?"

Pretty good? This elder didn't know every word to say. But he loved the Lord and loved the person he was talking to, and when he bore testimony of the Book of Mormon, that testimony went and touched the other person's heart. This power is explained in the Book of Mormon: "For when a man speaketh by the power of the Holy Ghost the power of the Holy Ghost carrieth it unto the hearts of the children of men" (2 Ne. 33:1).

You will enter the mission field to find, teach, and baptize. There is no hope for anyone on this earth unless they receive the covenants of the priesthood of God through baptism and the holy temple. You can be friendly and kind and loving, and that is good. But you must testify with power to bring people to Christ—the Spirit is that power.

Humility and Spiritual Growth

As part of the perfection process, the Book of Mormon instructs us that we must be humble or we will not learn (see 2 Ne. 9:42). And in Ether we are told that becoming humble is part of the process of learning, recognizing our weaknesses, and becoming strong and great in the Lord's hands. Humility is essential to that process: "And if men come unto me I will show unto them their weakness. I give unto men weakness that they may be humble; and my grace is sufficient for all men that humble themselves before me; for if they humble themselves before me, and have faith in me, then will I make weak things become strong unto them" (Ether 12:27).

Certainly the people in the Book of Mormon had a hard time with humility, and we have a hard time too. But we are told that when God loves a people, He chastens them (see Heb. 12:6). Chastening often results in humility, and we cannot grow without humility.

Humility is the beginning virtue or the precursor of all spiritual growth. Unless we are humble, we cannot grow. Elder Richard G. Scott describes this virtue in even greater detail:

> Humility is the precious, fertile soil of righteous character. It germinates the seeds of personal growth. When cultivated through the exercise of faith, pruned by repentance, and fortified by obedience and good works, such seeds produce the cherished fruit of spirituality (see Alma 26:22). Divine inspiration and power then result. Inspiration is to know the will of the Lord. Power is the capability to accomplish that inspired will (see D&C 43:15–16). Such power comes from God after we have done "all we can do" (2 Ne. 25:23).
>
> ("The Plan for Happiness and Exaltation," *Ensign,* Nov. 1981, 11.)

When Alma was teaching the Zoramites, many were humbled because they were cast out of the synagogue. And it was those who were cast out of the synagogue who listened to Alma and his message (see Alma 31–32). The wealthy and haughty Zoramites, those climbing up on the Rameumpton and praying, did not hear the word of God or feel the Spirit of the Lord. Humility is the key to our ability to change.

As missionaries, your hearts will resonate to President Lorenzo Snow's observation: "The Lord has not chosen the great and learned of the world to perform His work on the earth . . . but humble men [and women] devoted to His cause . . . who are willing to be led and guided by the Holy Spirit, and who will of necessity give the glory unto Him, knowing that of themselves they can do nothing" (*The Teachings of Lorenzo Snow,* ed. Clyde J. Williams [Salt Lake City: Bookcraft, 1989], 77).

Humility leads to righteousness and goodness. That's why I just love to be around missionaries, teaching them, because missionaries are so willing to accept the teachings of the Lord. I tingle when I think what a great honor and joy it is to work among the missionaries; their righteousness and willingness is inspiring and touching.

I can think of two missionaries in specific, a companionship I worked with when I was mission president. These two elders were my assistants. "President," they said, "we've only got a month left. We're training the new assistants and they're doing really well. President, please let us go teach and baptize." In other words, they didn't want the honor of being assistants to the president or any other honors of men. "Let us just go find and teach," they said. "President, we feel the power of God is upon us." And with that commitment and their strong desire, they went out and joyfully baptized twenty-three people in one month.

How was that possible? It happened because of the humility of two missionaries who gave themselves to the Lord and asked every day, "Father, what would thou have us do?" And then they went out and did it.

Of course, no matter how great we are, it doesn't mean we don't need to change. None of us are perfect. But it does mean that we are willing to serve, and that we are submitting to the Lord—giving Him the gift of our hearts. Whenever the people in the Book of Mormon were prideful or disobedient, the Lord would work with them to bring about humility so they could grow. Sometimes if the people were doing well, the Lord would send prophets who would exhort them to be better. Sometimes they became wicked, sinking into sinful behavior, and the Lord would still exhort them. Sometimes the people would change, and sometimes they wouldn't. Our challenge is to learn from their experiences and always be willing to change.

Overcoming Temptation

There are some things you need to be aware of. Temptation is real, and Satan desires to sift you as wheat. He does not want you to succeed in life, and especially does not want you to succeed as a missionary. You must pray every day to avoid and overcome temptation (see 3 Ne. 18:15, 18). Temptation is real. When you decide to serve a mission, you will face temptation. When you put in your papers, temptation becomes greater. When you get your call, temptation increases. You must remember the Lord needs you. You must overcome temptation with charity, with faith, with humility, with the word of God, and with the Spirit as we pray with all our heart, might, mind, and soul.

Cleansing Our Minds and Purifying Our Thoughts

There is an enduring principle for gaining the vision, cultivating the desire, and achieving the action that leads to results. That principle, put in simplest terms, is this: As [a man] thinketh in his heart, so is he (see Prov. 23:7). How can thoughts have such a powerful effect upon our behavior? Does the mind really control matter, even our attitude and behavior? The answer to this is a resounding yes! The process of thinking and mental exertion is the beginning of gaining the vision, desire, and action.

This is how the process works:

- A *Thought* (perceived or received) is an idea, a considertion, a reflection, a deliberation, a concept, an aspiration, a meditation, a pondering, about something. When this thought is . . .
- *Dwelled upon*, that is, brought to reside in your mind and to be continually present, such that you are engrossed in it and linger on it, this, in turn, . . .
- Creates a *Desire*, a want, a need, a penchant for, a wish, a willingness, a longing, an appetite, a passion or craving for something. When this is . . .
- *Encouraged*, which is to urge, help, inspire, promote, support, motivate, stimulate, strengthen, and to reassure, then it . . .
- Results in *Action*, which is to perform, execute, give effort, and to exert oneself. You actually do something. Your attitude has changed and you now behave in a new way. You are a result of your *thoughts*.

The catalyst for the transition from thoughts to desire is to dwell upon the thought. The catalyst for the transition from desire to action is to be continually encouraged i.e., to have the courage to act. The question now is one of initiative and self-mastery. Now that we understand the principle behind the thought process, the challenge rises: Where will your thoughts take you today?

When struggling with impure thoughts it takes effort and determination to overcome them. One day while I was discussing this problem with my friend Richard Heaton, who is presently Director of Training for the Provo MTC, I asked him to prepare a document concerning the following ideas on cleansing our minds and purifying our thoughts:

> As part of the repentance process, we have the difficult task of making restitution by cleansing our minds of the pictures, images, and thoughts we have placed there. You may be struggling with the same challenge the Lord identified in a latter-day revelation: "But your *mind* has been on the things of the earth more than on the things of me, your Maker, and the ministry whereunto you have been called; and you have not given heed unto my Spirit, and to those who were set over you (D&C 30:2, emphasis added).

> In order to receive the cleansing power of the Holy Ghost, you must "let virtue garnish [your] thoughts unceasingly" (see D&C 121:45). The following are some principles you may apply as you seek to cleanse your mind and receive His Spirit.

> **1. Keep the Commandments**
> The Lord revealed "that by *keeping the commandments* they might be *washed and cleansed* from all their sins, and receive the Holy Spirit" (D&C 76:52, emphasis added). The book of Proverbs promises, "Commit thy *works* unto the Lord, and thy *thoughts* shall be established" (Prov. 16:3, emphasis added).

> **2. Focus on Ordinances and Covenants, Especially the Sacrament**
> In addition to regular temple attendance, renewing your covenants through partaking of the sacrament and consciously striving to live up to those covenants will help keep your mind clean and worthy to partake of His Spirit. One of the conditions set forth in the sacramental prayers is that we will "always remember him" (see D&C 20:77, 79). The associated promise is that we will "have his Spirit to be with [us]." If we are striving

to remember the Savior, we will be unable to focus on things which rob us of the Spirit.

3. Fill Your Mind with Good and Virtuous Thoughts

The Apostle Paul taught, "Be not overcome of evil, but overcome evil with good" (Rom. 12:21). Be proactive in placing in your mind worthy, wholesome images and thoughts. Spend extra time each day reading and studying the scriptures. Read every issue of the Church magazines (*Ensign, New Era, Church News*). Learn to sing the hymns of the restoration. Memorize the words to your favorite hymns.

4. Do Not Let Any Unclean Thoughts Enter Your Mind

Be extremely careful of what you expose your eyes, ears, and mind to. Avoid the very appearance of evil. Like Nephi, you might pray, "Wilt thou make me that I may shake at the appearance of sin?" (2 Ne. 4:31). Realize that pornography, and other evil thoughts, can be in the form of books, pictures, movies, words, stories, or jokes. Destroy any easy access to this type of material (especially pornographic material). Destroy (don't just put away) any materials that offend the Spirit. Pray that God will warn you of approaching temptations and commit that as He does, you will do your part and avoid them. Commit now that when you return from your mission, you will continue to apply these principles by carefully screening and selecting the TV, books, movies, magazines, and language you will allow yourself to be exposed to.

5. Spend Time Each Day in Selfless Service

Your community has a homeless shelter that can use an extra set of hands. Deseret Industries needs help sorting or picking up donations. The welfare cannery can use an extra person. A ward member may be in a rest home or homebound and needs a visit. Rest homes can always use someone to visit people. Select a service opportunity and spend time each day. Through selfless service you can make restitution for self-gratifying transgressions.

6. Seek Individual Inspiration and Help from the Lord

In addition to applying general principles, the Lord will teach you specifically what you, as His son or daughter, can do to free yourself of unnecessary burdens. He knows you better than anyone else. He wants to make you clean. He will help you. Therefore, (1) pray for strength in all your personal prayers, and (2) read all verses in the Topical Guide under the topic "mind" and "thought." As you read each verse, prayerfully consider how that verse might apply to you, then set a goal to apply that verse.

As you feast upon the words of Christ, "the words of Christ will *tell you all things what ye should do*" (2 Ne. 32:3, emphasis added). As you receive the guidance of the Holy Ghost, "it will *show unto you all things what you should do*" (2 Ne. 32:5, emphasis added). Follow the promptings you receive.

The Promise

You are of great worth in the sight of God. He suffered death and the pain of all men that you might repent and come unto Him. His joy is great because you want to repent (see D&C 18:10–13). He wants to cleanse your mind of all that will keep His Spirit from being with you. He will make you clean (see D&C 88:74). He has promised, "Purify your hearts, and cleanse your hands and your feet before me, that I may make you clean; That I may testify unto your Father, and your God, and my God, that you are clean from the blood of this wicked generation; that I may fulfill this promise, this great and last promise, which I have made unto you, when I will" (D&C 88:74–75).

Here is a list of things to remember and do as you prepare to be a successful missionary for our Savior Jesus Christ—a pure disciple.

- Learn to work—work hard, be smart and persevere.
- Start sharing the gospel with those you meet.
- Practice speaking and giving talks. Learn to start up a conversation. Be friendly.
- Remember that you were born with self-esteem. You are a

child of God with a divine heritage and purpose.

- You can do anything in the strength of the Lord. You are responsible and accountable.
- Remember the Lord wants people committed and baptized (see 3 Ne. 11).
- Obey rules. To obey is greater than sacrifice (see 1 Sam. 15:22). Commandments and rules are designed to bring us happiness.
- Charity never faileth—love everyone.
- Learn missionary skills and practice coping in hard times.
- Search the scriptures and liken them unto yourself.
- Pray always—this is a MUST. The Lord will always do His part.
- Organize every needful thing, set goals, plan well, and follow through.
- Seek and gain a testimony though study and prayer and faithfully bear it.
- Learn to follow and be easily entreated—in short, seek humility (see Hel. 3:35).
- Seek the Spirit, rely on the Spirit, teach by the Spirit; do all things as directed by the Spirit.
- Open your mouth. Find people to teach.
- Be willing to work with members.
- Be bold, but not overbearing. Invite people to keep commitments as you keep yours.

As disciples, consider these points the Lord told Thomas B. Marsh found in Doctrine and Covenants 31. This scripture can become very meaningful to you and help in understanding your personal responsibility as you prepare to be a missionary.

- "Blessed are you because of your faith in my work" (v. 1).
- "Behold, you have had many afflictions . . . nevertheless, I will bless you and your family" (v. 2).
- "Lift up your heart and rejoice, for *the hour of your mission is come*" (v. 3; emphasis added).
- "Your tongue shall be loosed, and you shall declare glad tidings of great joy unto this generation" (v. 3).
- "Begin to preach from this time forth, yea, to reap in the

field which is white already to be burned" (v. 4).
- "Thrust in your sickle with all your soul" (v. 5).
- "Your sins are forgiven you, and you shall be laden with sheaves upon your back" (v. 5).
- "I will open the hearts of the people, and they will receive you" (v. 7).
- "And you shall strengthen them and prepare them" (v. 8).
- "It shall be given you by the Comforter what you shall do and whither you shall go" (v. 11).
- "Pray always, lest you enter into temptation and lose your reward" (v. 12).
- "Be faithful unto the end, and lo, I am with you" (v. 13).

This motivating section of the Doctrine and Covenants ends with this sobering reminder: *"These words are not of man nor of men, but of me, even Jesus Christ, your Redeemer, by the will of the Father. Amen"* (D&C 31:13; emphasis added). Our call is real, our commitment is eternal; we must become true disciples of Christ.

CONCLUSION

You are true disciples of Jesus Christ. You are examples to your fellowmen. I would like to describe you regarding the principles and values you not only live, but which guide your quest of bringing souls to Christ:

You are led by the Spirit in the "how to" of being obedient to the commandments. You are secure in knowing you are truly motivated by our Savior Jesus Christ, and you joy and glory in your instrumentality. You are not only guided by the Spirit, but you are empowered by a call from God through His holy prophet. This eternal verity makes you always think of others and how you can help them come to Christ, and likewise they in turn help others.

Your perception and vision of the work gives you a feeling of what we do and how to do it. You know you can do it in the strength of the Lord. You continually improve as you adapt to new approaches to missionary work with a positive attitude and a willing spirit. Your perception of yourself and the work, and the changes you have made, helps you become a mighty instrument in the hands of the Lord as you build up the kingdom of God.

The purpose of your mission is ingrained within your heart—bring souls to Christ through the waters of baptism. The end in mind is convert baptisms, and your mind is consumed with this thought. Each day you do the right things—you are obedient because you exercise faith and love God. And with time, effort, study, training, and by preparing every needful thing, you become a pure disciple of Jesus Christ. Your motive is pure—you love Christ and your fellowmen, and this releases your divine potential. You truly seek to enlighten and liberate the children of God with the gospel of Jesus Christ.

You grow step by step and are reinforced by the Spirit. You know you are doing the will of the Father. When opposition arises you respond by evaluating and diagnosing the situation, setting your goals, making your plans, and as President Kimball would say, by "doing it." This process is repeated as often as necessary to achieve your desired results.

As you become this great instrument in the hand of the Lord, you become the fulfillment of God's purpose for you on earth. You help build up the kingdom of God and assist in the Lord's work: "the immortality and eternal life of man" (see Moses 1:39). You bring joy to yourself and your fellowmen and cause our Heavenly Father's and our Savior's joy to be full because of your faith.

You, through humility and faith, can tap the strength of the Lord. You can become independent of the world as you gain strength in the Lord, that you might do all things whatsoever you are commanded. You truly become "even as He is" at those precious moments when you act and teach by the Spirit. You are His disciples. We are all one. We are on His errand. We shall not fail. We came to succeed. I testify of these eternal truths. They are of God and we are His anointed servants.

CHAPTER 5
THE LORD'S MISSIONARY: UNDERSTANDING THE DOCTRINES OF THE KINGDOM

As we strive to become worthy disciples of Christ, we develop a desire to know more about Him and His gospel; we begin to "hunger and thirst" after this righteousness (see 3 Ne. 12:6). Our further study of the gospel is vital. The discussions have recently been modified, allowing missionaries to teach more from their heart and by the Spirit, rather than from memorized dialogues. Our gospel knowledge is essential to have in our hearts. "Neither take ye thought beforehand what ye shall say; but treasure up in your minds continually the words of life, and it shall be given you in the very hour that portion that shall be meted unto every man" (D&C 84:85). We can see from this that if we have gospel knowledge, the Lord can give us inspiration at the very moment we need it.

GOSPEL KNOWLEDGE

Think about it. You want to go out on a mission, but do you think you'll really fully prepare in the MTC? Elder Daryl Garn related the following:

> Three months into my mission, a new missionary from Idaho was assigned to be my companion. We had been together only a few days when I realized something very significant: my new companion knew the gospel, while I only knew the discussions. How I wished that I had prepared to be a missionary as hard as I had prepared to be a basketball player. My companion had prepared for his mission throughout his life and was immediately a

valuable member of the team. How important it is for fathers and sons to work together on the basics in preparing for a mission.

("Preparing for Missionary Service," *Ensign,* May 2003, 46.)

It's important to understand many doctrines, principles, and teachings that will help you be a better representative of our Savior, Jesus Christ. If you study, understand, and appreciate the following doctrines, your own testimony will grow, and you will be a better instrument in the Lord's hands to help His children understand, appreciate, and accept the gospel in their lives. The following are some of the doctrines and principles taught in the first discussion you will need to understand.

The Atonement

The doctrine of the Atonement of Christ is the center of the gospel of Jesus Christ: "And this is the gospel, the glad tidings, which the voice out of the heavens bore record unto us—That he came into the world, even Jesus, to be crucified for the world, and to bear the sins of the world, and to sanctify the world, and to cleanse it from all unrighteousness" (D&C 76:40–41). This is the Atonement. He suffered that we might live. He sweat great drops of blood that we might be made pure. He died on the cross that we might live again. The principles of the Atonement that help us live again are the first principles of the gospel: faith in the Lord Jesus Christ, repentance through the Lord Jesus Christ, baptism and taking upon ourselves the name of Jesus Christ, and the receiving of the Holy Ghost.

I recommend a thorough, repeated study of 2 Nephi 9. By familiarizing yourself with this chapter, you'll understand the Atonement like you've never understood it before. Your gratitude will deepen. You'll recognize how tragic your destiny would have been had there been no Atonement.

Now, how can the Atonement help us? In Alma we read:

> And he shall go forth, suffering pains and afflictions and temptations of every kind; and this that the word might be fulfilled which saith he will take upon him the pains and the sicknesses of his people. And he will take upon him death, that he may loose the bands of death which bind his people; and he will take upon

him their infirmities, that his bowels may be filled with mercy, according to the flesh, that he may know according to the flesh how to succor his people according to their infirmities.

(Alma 7:11–12.)

Christ has been through it all: our sins, our pains, our sufferings, even our temptations. Of anyone, He knows what we need and how we can get through this life. And most importantly, He wants us to succeed.

The Atonement of Christ nurtures and blesses us through the grace of God. It helps us repent. We can overcome sin through repentance because of the grace of God and the atoning sacrifice. Sin separates us from the Father; we lose the Spirit, and we separate ourselves. The law of justice demands that sin be paid for. The law of mercy provides a way, through God's only begotten Son, to pay for our sins. Everything must be paid for. Earth life is not free; we knew that in our premortal life. Exaltation has a price—the grace of God after all we can do (see 2 Ne. 25:23). You see, every needful thing has a price, and the Atonement of Jesus Christ, our Savior, is the price He paid to fulfill the demands of divine justice.

Doctrine and Covenants 19:15–21 teaches us what price we must pay if we don't repent. If we do not repent, the Lord said we must suffer even as He has suffered; for the Atonement, as it relates to exaltation, requires that we must repent. The Atonement freely gives us all immortality, but eternal life—exaltation—comes only by *applying* the Atonement in our life, through repentance and endurance to the end.

Write in your journal today what you're going to do to show gratitude to the Savior for His atoning sacrifice. Your list of commitments can be lived every day, and you can make a covenant with the Lord in regard to your behavior because of His infinite, atoning sacrifice.

Faith

As discussed earlier, the doctrine of faith has three degrees: hope and belief, action, and power. You've read the definition of faith in Alma 32 and Hebrews 11: "Faith is the substance of things hoped for." That is the first degree of faith. James said, "I will shew thee my faith by my works"—meaning action (James 2:18). "The brother of

Jared said unto the mountain Zerin, Remove"—meaning power
(Ether 12:30). Faith is power, power to do all things. The earth was
created by faith. Faith is the vehicle of the priesthood. Faith is the
foundation of all righteousness. If you want to read more on faith as
power, then read the *Lectures on Faith* by the Prophet Joseph Smith,
and you'll begin to understand.

Joseph Smith taught that before we can exercise faith, we must
know the character of God—know that He exists, know that He is
perfect, know that we are actually living according to the will of God.
We cannot please God without faith (see Heb. 11:6). You cannot
exercise faith without love, and you can't have love without faith (see
Gal. 5:6). Faith, love, and obedience are intertwined. You cannot
separate one from another. The greater our faith, the more we will
love God, and if we love Him, we will obey Him. The Lord said, "if
you love me, keep my commandments" (see John 14:15). If we have
faith, we will mentally and spiritually exert ourselves and draw upon
the powers of heaven.

The question is left for us to answer: what kind of lives are we
living because of the Savior Jesus Christ? When we look at our lives,
remember, they are only a reflection of our conversion to Jesus Christ,
our faith in Him. When we exercise faith in Jesus Christ we will
repent and follow Him.

Prophets and Revelation

Another doctrine we need to understand concerns the prophets of
God, the spokesmen for the Lord Jesus Christ: "Surely the Lord God will
do nothing but he revealeth his secret unto his servants the prophets"
(Amos 3:7). Prophets speak for our Savior. They speak the words of
Christ. The Lord said, in Doctrine and Covenants 1:38, "Whether by
mine own voice or by the voice of my servants, it is the same." The
prophet functions as the President of the Church, the presiding high
priest, and the revelator of the Church for the Lord Jesus Christ. The
Quorum of the Twelve and Counsel of the First Presidency are also
prophets, seers, and revelators. They speak for the Lord.

In addition to that, every person should be a prophet for himself
regarding his own concerns. It was Moses who said, "would God that
all the Lord's people were prophets, and that the Lord would put his

spirit upon them" (Num. 11:29). Paul said we should "covet to prophesy" (1 Cor. 14:39). In other words, you can be a prophet for your own soul, receiving revelation from God on things *you* should do. (Remember always that the prophet of the Church is the only one who receives revelation for the Church and kingdom of God upon the earth.)

It is our duty to sustain the prophet, which means to support and follow what he has asked us to do. In the battle against the offender Amalek, the Israelites under Joshua prevailed as long as Moses' hands were outstretched on the top of the hill, supported on either side by Aaron and Hur (see Ex. 17:9–13). This wonderful example helps us realize how important Church members are regarding sustaining the prophet, and assisting in building up the kingdom of God.

How grateful we should be for a prophet, a living prophet of God. I bear testimony to you, that as we follow the prophets we will never be led astray.

The Divine Calling of Joseph Smith

How do you feel about the doctrine of the divine calling of the Prophet Joseph Smith? In the Doctrine and Covenants we read: "Joseph Smith, the Prophet and Seer of the Lord, has done more, save Jesus only, for the salvation of men in this world, than any other man that ever lived in it" (D&C 135:3). He was the prophet of the Restoration. He spoke for the Lord; he gave us the Book of Mormon, the Doctrine and Covenants, the Pearl of Great Price, and the inspired version of the Holy Bible. He established the kingdom as the Lord directed him.

We must bear testimony that Joseph Smith is the prophet of the Restoration. He holds the keys for the dispensation of the fullness of times. He is the prophet who stands at the head. When we think of all that the Prophet Joseph Smith has done, we will be grateful and recognize that our life is what it is today because of the revelations he received from our Savior by the power of the Holy Ghost.

Think of all the persecution that was heaped upon him. He was tarred and feathered and left for dead in Hyrum, Ohio. He was beaten, thrown in jail, and finally martyred. Can anyone doubt the blessings of the gospel in our lives because of what Joseph Smith did? He literally fulfilled the measure of his creation because of his integrity and love. In fact, when people ask why Joseph Smith was so great, the answer comes back that he was full of the love of Christ. Even the day after he was tarred and feathered he gave a talk on forgiveness and repentance, and some of the men who had done the deed were in attendance.

When you pray to Heavenly Father, you will know, as I know, that Joseph is the prophet of the Restoration, and the Church is led by a prophet today.

The Truthfulness of the Book of Mormon

The Book of Mormon is the keystone of our religion; the fullness of the gospel is in its printed pages. It is the word of God and the most correct book on earth. It will help us to get closer to God than any other book (see the Introduction to the Book of Mormon). The Book of Mormon is true, of that I testify. It is a record of the dealings of God with man. And the purpose of the book is to show the goodness and mercies of God to His people, and above all, to teach that Jesus is the Christ, the Son of the living God. As President Heber J. Grant said, "I am convinced in my own mind, my dear brethren and sisters, that this book, the Book of Mormon, is the greatest converter of men and women as to the divinity of the gospel of Jesus Christ. It is in every way a true witness of God, and it sustains the Bible and is in harmony with the Bible" (qtd. by Joseph L. Wirthlin, CR, Apr. 1947, 84).

The Book of Mormon—oh, how I love the book. For twenty-seven glorious years I've had the privilege of teaching that book at Brigham Young University and the Orem Institute of Religion. It has made a difference in my family's life. When we read it on a daily basis, it helps us to live the word of God. There are legions of people who have read the book and then requested baptism because of the power of its words. The Spirit carries truthfulness unto the hearts of the people. And the true seekers, the Lord's elect, will believe.

When you study the Book of Mormon today, remember to apply its teachings to your own life. Every teaching in the Book of Mormon is to be applied to life. The prophet Nephi said, "I did liken all scriptures unto us . . . for our profit and learning" (1 Ne. 19:23). When studied this way, the Book of Mormon works in people's lives. It brings them unto Christ. President Marion G. Romney once said, "The Book of Mormon is the most effective piece of missionary literature we have" ("Drink Deeply from the Divine Fountain," *Improvement Era*, June 1960, 435).

When we ourselves, or someone to whom we are teaching the gospel, accepts the Book of Mormon as true, consider what happens:

1. If we accept the Book of Mormon, we accept Joseph Smith as a prophet of God.
2. If Joseph Smith was a prophet of God, the First Vision was a reality.
3. If the First Vision was a reality, God did establish this kingdom on earth, and the priesthood was in fact restored to the earth.
4. If the priesthood of God was restored through angels under the direction of God, the Doctrine and Covenants, Pearl of Great Price, and other LDS scriptures and revelations are valid.
5. If the priesthood and the accompanying ordinances were restored, the organization we call The Church of Jesus Christ of Latter-day Saints is the institution of God restored on earth today—in *fact*, not only in *name*.
6. If Christ's Church is restored, it is led by His prophets, to whom He continues to reveal His mind and will—His purposes for His children on earth.
7. Through the Church, we become aware of our eternal heritage and of eternal relationships and future possibilities.
8. All of these things strengthen our witness that Jesus is the Christ and that there is purpose to the Creation, to His ministry, to all the unfolding of truth, and to all eternity.

The Holy Ghost

When the Savior was preaching to the people of the Nephite nation, they prayed for that which they desired more than anything else, that they might have the gift of the Holy Ghost (see 3 Ne. 19:9). Why did they pray for the Holy Ghost? Why did they desire to have it so much? Because, as Elder Bruce R. McConkie tells us, "He is the Comforter, Testator, Revelator, Sanctifier, Holy Spirit, Holy Spirit of Promise, Spirit of Truth, Spirit of the Lord, and Messenger of the Father and the Son, and His companionship is the greatest gift that mortal man can enjoy" (Bruce R. McConkie, *Mormon Doctrine*, 2nd ed. [Salt Lake City: Bookcraft, 1966], 359).

In addition to faith, love, and obedience, four specific things will invite the Spirit into our lives: (1) searching the scriptures, (2) fasting and praying, (3) giving righteous service, and (4) building up the kingdom of God.

We cannot have the Spirit without righteousness, and we cannot teach save we have the Spirit (see D&C 42:14). The Holy Ghost must be with us as we teach. The Holy Ghost will bear witness to anyone that the gospel is true. In Galatians, we read about receiving the spirit of love, peace, joy, long-suffering, gentleness, goodness, faith, meekness, and temperance (see Gal. 5:22–23); all these are fruits of the Spirit. When we feel good, we are feeling the influence of the Spirit. In Doctrine and Covenants 11:12–13, the Lord talks about the Spirit again. He says that the Holy Ghost will lead us to do good, to be humble, to deal justly, to judge righteously. It will enlighten our souls and bring us joy. Yes, the fruits of the Spirit will help us recognize the Spirit and to identify Him for others so we can help them know the gospel is true.

Recognizing the Spirit of God in our life is no different than asking investigators to recognize the Spirit—don't look beyond the mark; you need not have a burning bush. A simple feeling of peace and a desire to do good should be enough. The Holy Ghost will be a comfort and a guide, and direct you in every way. The Lord will not leave you alone as you prepare every needful thing to bless the lives of your fellowmen and build up the kingdom of God.

Prayer

Sometimes missionaries say, "Well, I just don't get an answer, President," or "My investigators just don't get answers when they pray." Heavenly Father teaches us that we must study things out to know of their truthfulness; then we need to make a decision (see D&C 9:7–9). Then we take that decision to the Lord and He will cause our bosom to burn. Sometimes we'll just feel peace, as the Lord pointed out to Oliver Cowdrey: "Did I not speak peace to your mind?" He asked, explaining this as an answer to prayer (see D&C 6:23). Remember all those other feelings of the Spirit? We will feel good, we will be humble, and we'll have a desire to deal justly with others. These are the feelings that will tell you that the gospel is true. But, as with Oliver in section 9, we can't just ask. The Lord says, "You took no thought save it was to ask me" (v. 7). We must ask with real intent, having faith, having done the things we need to do, and then our prayers will be answered. In other words, prayers are answered when we do our part. We just cannot say, "Give me, give me, give me," but we must come before our Lord, our God, with all our heart, might, mind, and strength, having faith with real intent, and then He will answer our prayers, either directly or through others.

Prayer is communicating with our Heavenly Father in the name of Jesus Christ. That is the way you pray. It is through and in the name of Jesus Christ. In 3 Nephi 18, we note that the Savior continually told the Nephites to pray in His own name; that is so we may know that it is through Jesus Christ, our advocate and mediator, that God our Father helps us. Know that God hears and answers prayers. Pray with real intent, without vain repetitions, with a sincere heart, having faith, and with every needful thing in place.

We can pray standing up, we can be walking along on the street, we can be leaning against a building. The Lord said that when we cease our prayers, we should have a prayer in our hearts (see 3 Ne. 20:1). Our prayers must be sent up to heaven continually. Prayer is the very essence of knowing and worshiping our Heavenly Father. It is "the act by which the will of the Father and the will of the child are brought into correspondence with each other" (Bible Dictionary, "Prayer," 752). We must take the time to know our Father, and His will, through prayer.

Always remember to use *Thee, Thou,* and *Thine* to show reverence. Remember always to pray to have the courage to do the will of the Father.

Prayer is our way of communicating with heaven. It is an exchange of love with Heavenly Father. It is an earth child checking in with his Heavenly Father. It is a servant seeking direction, comfort, and strength from the Master.

The first part of your prayer, after calling upon Heavenly Father, may be to keep very still and wait for that closeness to come upon you. Listen to your heart and reach with your mind until you feel different from when you knelt down. That's when your spirit has connected with heaven.

Recall the incident in the mission of Jesus when He was coming into Jerusalem and the crowds were pressing about Him, trying to get close to Him. A woman who had been diseased for twelve years felt that if she could but touch Jesus' clothing she would be made whole. So she found the hem of His garment and touched it. Jesus, even in the midst of the crowd, felt her touch His clothing. Her touch was different from the press of the crowds. She had connected in faith, and He knew it. That's how sensitive He was; that's how powerful the Spirit is. The woman was immediately healed.

That is what it means to stay on your knees until you "feel different." To spin off a memorized prayer or mumble a quick message to God is not the same as:

- Communicating in humility with God the Father in the name of His Son, Jesus.
- Having an exchange of love.
- Sharing deep feelings of gratitude and need.
- Cleansing your soul through confession.
- Pleading for forgiveness.
- Witnessing your resolve to do better.
- Praying for those who despitefully use you.
- Asking for guidance to find people waiting to be taught.
- Seeking understanding of gospel principles as recorded in the scriptures.
- Promising obedience.
- Explaining your need for strength to endure.
- Seeking facility in a language and in learning teaching material.
- Searching for ways to love others.
- Crying out for confidence to do God's will.
- Desiring power to heal and bless.
- Yearning before God for peace on earth and holiness among men.

The scriptures are full of helpful counsel on prayer. A missionary really needs to know the wisdom in daily personal prayer, the miracle in group prayer, the strength and learning in urgent prayer, the growth and sense of well-being in prayers of gratitude.

The scriptures have this to say about prayer:

- "Pray always, lest ye enter into temptation and lose your reward" (D&C 31:12).
- "You must study it out in your mind; then you must ask me if it be right, and if it is right I will cause that your bosom shall burn within you" (D&C 9:8).
- "Pray always, that you may come off conqueror" (D&C 10:5).
- "Pray always, and I will pour out my Spirit upon you" (D&C 19:38).
- "The prayers of the faithful shall be heard, and all those who have dwindled in unbelief shall not be forgotten" (2 Ne. 26:15).
- "Pray unto the Father with all the energy of heart" (Moro. 7:48).
- "Love endureth by diligence unto prayer" (Moro. 8:26).
- "If any of you lack wisdom, let him ask of God, that giveth to all men liberally, and upbraideth not; and it shall be given him" (James 1:5).
- "But let him ask in faith, nothing wavering. For he that wavereth is like a wave of the sea driven with the wind and tossed" (James 1:5–6).
- "Be thou humble; and the Lord thy God shall lead thee by the hand, and give thee answer to thy prayers" (D&C 112:10).
- "Draw near unto me and I will draw near unto you; seek me diligently and ye shall find me; ask, and ye shall receive; knock, and it shall be opened unto you" (D&C 88:63).

Many people think of chapter 34 of Alma as the definitive statement concerning this life—now is the time to prepare to meet God. The notes at the beginning of the chapter seem to concur. However, it is interesting to note that much of this chapter has to do with prayer and the way to communicate with God *before* actually meeting Him. Read again this exciting scripture, particularly verses 17 through 27. Note how much prayer is to be a part of our lives. The times we are commanded to "pray always" in the scriptures are innumerable. Here are just a few more paraphrased examples:

- Pray always to avoid temptation (see 3 Ne. 18:15–18).

- Pray always and not faint before performing for the Lord (see 2 Ne. 32:9).
- Pray always to know the mysteries of God and to bring thousands to repentance (see Alma 26:22).
- Pray in your heart continually for the welfare of self and others (see Alma 34:27).
- Pray always lest the wicked one remove you out of your place (see D&C 93:49).
- Pray always vocally and in your heart while proclaiming the gospel (see D&C 81:3).
- Continue in prayer and fasting from this time forward (see D&C 88:76).
- Pray always and be believing, and all things will work together for your good (see D&C 90:24).
- Pray always lest the wicked one have power over you (see D&C 93:49–50).
- Pray always lest you lose your reward (see D&C 31:12).
- Pray always to understand the scriptures (see D&C 32:4).
- Pray always to be ready for the Second Coming (see D&C 33:17).
- Continue in prayer (see Rom. 2:12).
- Pray always in the Spirit for all Saints (part of taking on the armor of God) (see Eph. 6:18).

Testimony

No one can really be a minister of the Lord Jesus Christ, except he has a testimony that Jesus is the Christ. Our testimony, when truly borne, is borne by the power of the Holy Ghost. That makes our testimonies as strong as any man's upon the earth, because true testimonies are only borne by the power of the Spirit. So when we are bearing witness of the truthfulness of the gospel, the truthfulness of the Book of Mormon, the truthfulness of the prophet, the truthfulness of the teachings, the truthfulness of the kingdom of God on the earth, we do this by the power and authority of the Holy Ghost. The Holy Ghost is the testator, He is the revelator, and it is only by the Holy Ghost that we can testify to the truthfulness of the knowledge that Jesus is the Christ, the Son of God, and that

The Church of Jesus Christ of Latter-day Saints is the true kingdom of God on the earth.

Can you see now that one of the most priceless possessions we have is our testimony? Bearing testimony is testifying of revealed eternal truths in the gospel of Jesus Christ.

How do we get a testimony? Study, pray, live it, and bear it. Isn't that interesting? What do we ask investigators to do? Study, pray, and live the commandments. You see, we do everything by eternal truths. Nothing we ask of investigators is by happenstance. How many prophets have preached those same doctrines? To gain a testimony we must study, pray, live it, and bear it, and then we'll know. President Hinckley reaffirms this for us: "If there are any [of you] lacking that testimony, you can get it; and you must get it. . . . The Lord has said that he that doeth the will of the Father shall know of the doctrine, 'whether it be of God, or whether I speak of myself' (John 7:17)." (*Teachings of Gordon B. Hinckley*, 648.)

When we bear our testimonies, they are strengthened because we're invoking the Holy Ghost. The more experiences we have with the Holy Ghost, the stronger our testimonies become. Sometimes it is given to us to have a testimony on the words of others (see D&C 46:14); sometimes we have to do that until our testimony is strong enough. Everything we have is a gift of God, and this testimony that we possess, no matter how small, or how great, is a gift from God. Think of the times when other people's testimonies have affected yours. Think of the times other people have been affected by your testimony. The greatest converting power is the power of testimony, the word of God as given by the Spirit. Testimony is the purest form of the word; the power of the word has greater power to change men's lives than anything else (see Alma 31:5). Testify. Truth without testimony is hollow. The gospel is true, and we are the instruments through which the Lord works to share the truth with every nation, kindred, tongue, and people.

Familiarize Yourself with the Scriptures

The following chart is a list of scriptures my dear friend Russ Greiner made to aid him in his gospel study. You can create a useful cross-reference guide within your own sciptures to help you obtain knowledge of the scriptures, and assist you in preaching the gospel. After the chart below, follow the instructions for maximizing your familiarity with the scriptures.

CHRIST

2 Nephi 9:41
2 Nephi 26:33
Omni 1:26
Mosiah 3:8
Mosiah 3:17
Mosiah 5:13
Helaman 5:12
3 Nephi 27:13–14
Ether 12:41
Moroni 10:32
D&C 19:23
Moses 1:39
Moses 6:63
Matthew 1:21
Matthew 11:5
Matthew 11:28–30
Matthew 18:20
Matthew 23:37
Luke 2:1–17
Luke 2:52
John 3:16
John 14:6
John 15:5
Romans 8:38–39
1 Corinthians 10:1–4
Colossians 1:14–15
Hebrews 13:8
Revelation 1:8
Revelation 3:20
Revelation 22:12–13
Exodus 6:2–3
Isaiah 7:14
Isaiah 9:6
Isaiah 43:11
Zechariah 12:10

ATONEMENT

2 Nephi 2:6–7
2 Nephi 2:8
2 Nephi 2:26
2 Nephi 9:21–22
2 Nephi 25:26
Mosiah 3:7
Mosiah 3:19
Alma 7:11–13
Alma 11:40–41
Alma 34:8–9
Alma 42:15
D&C 18:11–12
D&C 19:16–19
D&C 45:3–5
D&C 76:40–42
D&C 88:33
Luke 22:42–44
John 15:13
Romans 3:23–25
1 Peter 1:18–20
1 John 1:7
1 John 2:1–2
Isaiah 53:3–5

GODHEAD

3 Nephi 11:3, 7
D&C 130:22–23
Matthew 16:13–18
John 5:19
John 8:17–18
John 14:8–9
John 16:27–29
John 17:3–5
John 17:20–22
Acts 7:55–56
1 Timothy 2:3–6
Hebrews 1:1–3
James 3:9
Genesis 1:26–27
Genesis 5:1–3

Gods

John 10:34–35
Romans 8:16–17
1 Corinthians 8:5–6
Philippians 2:5–6
1 John 3:2
Revelation 1:6
Genesis 3:22
Deuteronomy 10:17
Psalms 82:6

PLAN OF SALVATION

Premortal Life

Alma 13:3
Ether 3:15–17
D&C 93:28–29,36
Moses 3:5
Abraham 3:22–23
John 1:1–4,14
John 6:38
John 8:58
John 17:3–5
Acts 17:29
Ephesians 3:9
Colossians 1:14–15
Hebrews 12:9
Revelation 12:7–9
Numbers 16:22
1 Kings 22:19
Job 1:6
Job 32:8
Job 38:4–7
Jeremiah 1:4–5

The Veil

1 Corinthians 13:12
Isaiah 25:7

The Purpose of Life

2 Nephi 2:11
2 Nephi 2:25,27
2 Nephi 10:23–24
2 Nephi 25:23

2 Nephi 28:7–9
Alma 34:31–32
D&C 14:7
D&C 93:33–34
D&C 93:36
D&C 130:18–19
D&C 131:6
Abraham 3:25
Matthew 6:33
Matthew 16: 24–26
Matthew 24:13
Romans 6:23
1 Corinthians 10:13
2 Corinthians 5:7
Galatians 6:7–9
Philippians 2:12
1 Thessalonians 5:21–22

The Spirit World

Alma 40:11–12
Luke 23:43
John 3:13
John 5:25
John 20:16–17
1 Corinthians 15:29
1 Peter 3:18–19
1 Peter 4:6

Resurrection

1 Nephi 15:34
Alma 11:43–44
Alma 40:23
Alma 41:10
3 Nephi 11:7–15
D&C 88:15–16
D&C 130:2
Matthew 27:52–53
Matthew 28:1–8
Luke 24:1–9
Luke 24:36–39
John 5:28–29
John 10:17–18
John 11:25
John 14:1–2
John 20:26–29
Acts 24:15
Romans 6:9–10
1 Corinthians 2:9
1 Corinthians 15:5–6
1 Corinthians 15:20–22
1 Corinthians 15:40–42
1 Corinthians 15:44–45
1 Corinthians 15:55
2 Corinthians 12:2,4
1 Timothy 6:7
Revelation 20:6
Job 19:25–27
Ecclesiastes 12:7
Isaiah 26:19

Judgment
1 Nephi 10:20–21
Mosiah 4:30
Alma 12:14,16
Mormon 9:4
D&C 72:3–4
D&C 76:111–112
D&C 121:29
D&C 137:9
Matthew 25:21
John 5:22
John 5:30
2 Corinthians 3:9
Revelation 20:12

SECOND COMING
D&C 45:26–27
D&C 101:32–33
Acts 1:9–11
1 Thessalonians 4:16–17

FAITH
1 Nephi 7:12
1 Nephi 17:50
2 Nephi 25:23
Jacob 4:6
Mosiah 4:9–10
Alma 30:44
Alma 32:21
Alma 37:6
Ether 12:6
Ether 12:27
Moroni 7:33
D&C 81:6
D&C 88:118
D&C 90:24
Matthew 21:21–22
Mark 9:23
Romans 8:31
Romans 10:17
Philippians 4:13
2 Timothy 4:7–8
Hebrews 11:1
Hebrews 11:6
James 1:3
James 2:14–20,26
Joshua 1:9
Psalms 19:1
Proverbs 3:5–6

Calling & Election
D&C 67:10
D&C 88:68
D&C 93:1
D&C 131:5
2 Peter 1:10

HOPE
Ether 12:4
Moroni 7:41
1 Corinthians 15:19

CHARITY
Moroni 7:47
Matthew 5:44
Matthew 7:12
Matthew 22:36–39
John 13:34–35
Romans 8:28
1 Corinthians 13:1–13
1 Peter 4:8
1 John 4:7–8
1 John 4:20–21
Deuteronomy 6:5–7

REPENTANCE
Mosiah 4:2–3
Mosiah 26:29–30
Alma 22:18
Alma 34:17
Alma 34:34–35
Alma 36:16–21
D&C 1:31–32
D&C 18:10,13–14
D&C 58:42–43
Luke 9:62
Acts 17:30
2 Corinthians 7:10
Philippians 3:13–14
Titus 2:11–12
Hebrews 6:6
2 Peter 3:9
1 John 1:7–9
Psalms 51:10–11
Proverbs 28:13
Isaiah 1:18
Isaiah 43:25
Ezekiel 18:21–22

BAPTISM
2 Nephi 9:23–24
2 Nephi 31:4–12
2 Nephi 31:13
2 Nephi 31:17,19–20
Mosiah 18:8–10
Alma 7:14–15
3 Nephi 11:33–34
3 Nephi 27:19–20
Ether 4:18–19
Moroni 6:2–4
Moroni 8:25
D&C 20:37
D&C 20:73–74
D&C 22:1–4
D&C 68:25
D&C 84:74
Matthew 3:13–17
Mark 1:4
Luke 3:3
John 3:5
Acts 2:37–38
Acts 8:12
Acts 8:36–38

Acts 19:1–6
Acts 22:16
Romans 6:3–5
Galatians 3:27
Colossians 2:12

Infant Baptism
Moroni 8:10–12,20
Moses 6:54

Baptism for the Dead
D&C 128:22
1 Corinthians 15:29

HOLY GHOST
1 Nephi 4:6
1 Nephi 10:17
1 Nephi 17:45
2 Nephi 32:5
2 Nephi 33:1–2
Jacob 4:13
Mosiah 2:9
Mosiah 5:2
Alma 5:46
Alma 10:6
Helaman 5:30
Moroni 7:16–19
Moroni 10:4–5
D&C 6:22–23
D&C 8:2–3
D&C 9:7–9
D&C 11:12–13
D&C 50:24
D&C 63:64
D&C 76:12
D&C 84:85
D&C 85:6
D&C 93:24
Matthew 10:20
Luke 24:32
John 14:26
John 14:27
Acts 8:14–20
1 Corinthians 2:11–14
1 Corinthians 12:3
Galatians 5:22
1 Kings 19:11–12
Joel 2:28

BORN AGAIN
Mosiah 5:7
Mosiah 27:25–26
Alma 5:14–16,26–27
Alma 7:14
Moses 6:59–60
John 3:3–5
1 John 5:4–5
Ezekiel 36:26–27

PRAYER
1 Nephi 15:8–9
2 Nephi 32:8–9
Enos 1:4
Alma 37:35–37
Helaman 3:35
Helaman 10:4–5
3 Nephi 18:18
3 Nephi 18:20
3 Nephi 18:21
3 Nephi 19:9
Mormon 9:27
Moroni 7:9
Moroni 7:48
D&C 9:7–9
D&C 10:5
D&C 25:12
D&C 42:61
D&C 46:30
D&C 50:29–30
D&C 78:19
D&C 88:63–65
D&C 101:7–8
D&C 112:10
D&C 136:28
Matthew 6:9–13
Matthew 7:7–8
Matthew 21:22
1 Thessalonians 5:16–18
James 1:5–6
James 4:3
James 5:16
1 John 3:22
Numbers 6:24–26
Job 33:14–16
Psalms 23:1–6
Psalms 118:24
Proverbs 21:13

APOSTASY
Alma 24:30
Joseph Smith History 1:19
Matthew 15:8–9
Matthew 21:43
Matthew 24:4–5 & 23–24
Acts 20:29–30
1 Corinthians 1:10–14
Galatians 1:6–8
2 Thessalonians 2:1–3
1 Timothy 4:1–3
2 Timothy 3:1–7
2 Timothy 4:3–4
2 Peter 2:21
Jude 1:10
Deuteronomy 4:28
Isaiah 24:5
Isaiah 60:2
Amos 8:11–12

RESTORATION
D&C 1:29–30
D&C 13
D&C 27:12–13
Joseph Smith History 1:5–8,11–15,
16–17
Matthew 17:11–13
Acts 3:19–21
Ephesians 1:10
Revelation 14:6–7
Isaiah 2:2–5
Isaiah 11:12
Isaiah 29:13–14
Daniel 2:44–45
Malachi 4:5–6

BOOK OF MORMON
1 Nephi 6:4
1 Nephi 13:40
2 Nephi 3:12
2 Nephi 28:29–30
2 Nephi 29:3,8
2 Nephi 33:5
2 Nephi 33:10–11
Mormon 9:7–8
Moroni 10:3–5
D&C 17:6
D&C 20:5–12
D&C 84:57
John 10:14–16
3 Nephi 15:21
2 Corinthians 13:1
Revelation 14:6–7
Genesis 49:22–26
Deuteronomy 4:2
2 Kings 19:31
1 Chronicles 5:1–2
Psalms 85:11
Isaiah 29:11–12
Isaiah 29:13–14
Isaiah 29:17–19,24
Ezekiel 37:15–17

PROPHETS
2 Nephi 3:14–15
Jacob 4:8
Jacob 7:11
D&C 1:14,17
D&C 1:38
D&C 5:10
D&C 20:25–26
D&C 21:4–5
D&C 35:17
D&C 68:3–4
D&C 76:22–23
D&C 122:1–2
D&C 135:3
Moses 1:11

Joseph Smith History 1:25
Matthew 7:15–16
Matthew 10:41
Mark 2:22
Luke 24:25
1 Corinthians 9:1
Hebrews 9:16–17
Revelation 19:10
Genesis 17:1
Genesis 32:30
Exodus 24:9–11
Exodus 33:11
Numbers 11:29
Numbers 12:6–8
2 Chronicles 20:20
Isaiah 6:1,5
Jeremiah 28:9
Amos 3:7
Malachi 3:1–2

PRIESTHOOD & CHURCH GOVERNMENT
Jacob 1:19
Mosiah 21:33
Alma 4:10
3 Nephi 27:7
3 Nephi 27:8
3 Nephi 27:21
Moroni 6:4
D&C 6:6
D&C 13
D&C 26:2
D&C 27:12–13
D&C 42:11
D&C 42:42
D&C 43:8–9
D&C 64:29
D&C 72:3–4
D&C 81:5
D&C 82:14
D&C 84:33–41
D&C 105:5
D&C 107:18–19
D&C 107:99–100
D&C 108:7
D&C 115:4
D&C 121:33–46
Moses 7:18
Matthew 15:24
Matthew 16:19
Mark 3:14–15
Luke 6:13–16
Luke 10:1,17
John 15:16
Acts 1:22–26
Acts 2:47
Acts 6:6–8
Acts 8:18–20

(Priesthood & Church Government continued)
Acts 10:34–35
Acts 13:2–3
Acts 19:1–6
Acts 19:13–16
1 Corinthians 11:2
1 Corinthians 12:27–31
Ephesians 2:19–20
Ephesians 4:4–6
Ephesians 4:11–14
Ephesians 5:23
Titus 1:5
Hebrews 5:4–6
Hebrews 5:8–10
Hebrews 7:11–12
James 5:14–15
1 Peter 2:9
Numbers 27:18–19

COMMANDMENTS

Ten Commandments
Exodus 20:3–17

Chastity
Jacob 2:35
Alma 39:5
Alma 39:11
Moroni 9:9
D&C 42:22–25
D&C 59:6
1 Corinthians 6:9–10
1 Corinthians 6:19–20
Proverbs 6:32
Proverbs 12:4

Sabbath
D&C 59:9–10
Exodus 20:8–11

Tithing
D&C 64:23
Malachi 3:8–10

Word of Wisdom
D&C 89:18–21
1 Corinthians 3:16–17

Judging
Moroni 7:16–19
Matthew 7:1–5
1 Samuel 16:7

Commandments (General)
D&C 29:34–35
D&C 88:121,123,124–125
Psalms 19:7–8

OBEDIENCE
1 Nephi 3:7
1 Nephi 17:3
2 Nephi 9:28–29
Jacob 4:10
Mosiah 2:41
Mosiah 5:5
Alma 7:23–24
Alma 37:35
Alma 57:21
D&C 14:7
D&C 58:21
D&C 59:21
D&C 59:23
D&C 64:34
D&C 82:3
D&C 82:10
D&C 84:44
D&C 130:20–21
D&C 132:5
Moses 5:6–8
Abraham 3:25
Matthew 5:3–12
Matthew 6:22
Matthew 7:13–14
Matthew 7:21–23
Luke 6:46
John 7:16–17
John 13:17
John 14:15
James 1:22
1 John 2:3–4
1 Samuel 15:22
Ecclesiastes 12:13
Isaiah 64:8

SERVICE
Jacob 2:18–19
Mosiah 2:17
Mosiah 2:21–22
D&C 42:29
D&C 58:26–28
D&C 59:5
D&C 76:5–6
D&C 98:13
Matthew 6:24
Matthew 7:12
Matthew 10:39
Matthew 23:11–12
Matthew 25:40
Acts 10:38
James 1:27
1 Peter 2:15
Joshua 24:15

MISSIONARY WORK
1 Nephi 13:37
Mosiah 28:3
Alma 17:2–3

Alma 17:16
Alma 26:11–12
Alma 26:16
Alma 26:22
Alma 29:1–2
Alma 29:8
Alma 29:9
Alma 31:5
Alma 31:34–35
Alma 36:24
Alma 38:10–12
3 Nephi 5:13
3 Nephi 7:18
D&C 1:4–5
D&C 4:1–7
D&C 6:9
D&C 11:20–21
D&C 12:8
D&C 14:8
D&C 15:6
D&C 18:15–16
D&C 19:29–31
D&C 27:15–18
D&C 29:7
D&C 31:5
D&C 34:6–10
D&C 35:13–14
D&C 42:6–7
D&C 43:15–16
D&C 50:13–14
D&C 52:9
D&C 58:47
D&C 60:13
D&C 63:58
D&C 84:88
D&C 84:106
D&C 88:81–82
D&C 90:11
D&C 100:5–8
D&C 103:36
D&C 112:19
D&C 123:12–13
Matthew 9:37–38
Matthew 19:29
Matthew 24:14
Matthew 28:19–20
Mark 6:7–12
Mark 16:15–18
Luke 22:32
Acts 1:6–8
Acts 5:38–39
Romans 8:31
Romans 10:15
1 Corinthians 3:6
1 Corinthians 9:16–18
James 5:19–20
Jeremiah 3:14
Jeremiah 16:16

TESTIMONY
Alma 5:45–46
D&C 60:2–3
D&C 62:3
D&C 76:79
Matthew 10:32–33
Matthew 16:15–18
John 7:16–17
John 8:31–32
Romans 1:16
1 Corinthians 12:3
2 Timothy 1:7–8
1 Peter 3:15
Revelation 3:15–16
Revelation 19:10

EXAMPLE
2 Nephi 31:9
2 Nephi 31:16
Alma 48:17
3 Nephi 12:48
3 Nephi 18:24
3 Nephi 27:27
Matthew 5:14–16
Matthew 5:48
John 13:15
1 Timothy 4:12

SCRIPTURE STUDY
1 Nephi 15:24
1 Nephi 19:23
2 Nephi 4:15
2 Nephi 32:3
Helaman 3:29
D&C 1:37
D&C 6:2
D&C 18:34–36
D&C 68:3–4
John 5:39
John 20:31
John 21:25
Acts 1:1–2
2 Corinthians 3:3
Galatians 1:11–12
2 Timothy 3:16–17
2 Peter 1:19–21
Joshua 1:8
Psalms 119:103
Psalms 119:105
Jeremiah 20:9

TEACHING
2 Nephi 33:1
Mosiah 23:14
Alma 38:10–12
D&C 42:12
D&C 42:14
D&C 50:21–23
D&C 88:77–78
D&C 88:122

Acts 8:30–31
Romans 2:21
Romans 10:14

SACRAMENT
Moroni 6:5–6
D&C 20:77,79
Luke 22:19–20
1 Corinthians 11:23–30

TEMPLES
D&C 88:119
D&C 97:15–16
Psalms 24:3–4
Isaiah 2:2–5

MARRIAGE & FAMILY
Mosiah 4:14–15
3 Nephi 22:13
D&C 49:15
D&C 49:16
D&C 68:25
D&C 93:40
D&C 131:1–3
D&C 132:19
Mark 10:6–9
Mark 10:14
1 Corinthians 7:3
1 Corinthians 11:11
Ephesians 5:25
Ephesians 6:4
1 Timothy 5:8
Hebrews 13:4
3 John 1:4
Genesis 18:19
Proverbs 18:22
Proverbs 22:1
Proverbs 22:6
Proverbs 31:10–11,26,28

THOUGHTS
Mosiah 4:30
Alma 12:14
D&C 6:36
D&C 84:85
D&C 121:45–46
Proverbs 15:26
Proverbs 23:7
Isaiah 55:8–9

FORGIVENESS
D&C 64:9–10
Matthew 18:21–22
Luke 6:37

SELF–DISCIPLINE
Matthew 18:3
Romans 12:21
Ephesians 4:26
Ephesians 4:31–32

James 1:8
James 1:19
Proverbs 15:1
Proverbs 16:18
Proverbs 16:32
Proverbs 25:28

UNITY
4 Nephi 1:15–17
D&C 38:24,27
Moses 7:18
Mark 3:23–25

AMERICA
Mosiah 29:26–27
Ether 2:12
Matthew 21:43
Proverbs 14:34
Proverbs 29:2

ADVERSITY
Alma 36:3
D&C 58:3–4
D&C 121:7–8
D&C 122:7–8
D&C 136:31
Romans 5:3–5

SIN/DISOBEDIENCE
3 Nephi 6:18
D&C 82:7
Titus 1:16
Hebrews 10:26
James 4:17
1 John 3:4
Proverbs 6:16–19
Isaiah 5:20
Hosea 8:7

DEVIL
2 Nephi 28:20–22
3 Nephi 11:29
D&C 10:27
Moses 4:4
Revelation 12:7–9
Revelation 13:7

You can create your own cross-reference guide within your scriptures by simply finding the first scripture on the list of any of the preceding categories. Then, in the margins of your scriptures, next to that particular verse, write the scripture reference for the second verse on the list in that same category. That way, no matter what scripture you turn to on any given topic, there is another one referenced right where you need it. So, for example, on the preceding chart under the section "Apostasy," the first listed scripture is Alma 24:30. The second source listed is Joseph Smith History 1:19. So, next to Alma 24:30 in your scriptures, simply write the word "Apostasy" and then the reference to "JS–H 1:19" next to it.

CONCLUSION

When we come to understand and appreciate the doctrines and principles of the gospel, we will be filled with gratitude. Gratitude is a catalyst for change. Our attitudes and behaviors will change as these doctrines are integrated into our lives and become part of our very being. As President Boyd K. Packer has said, "The study of the doctrines of the gospel will improve behavior quicker than a study of behavior will improve behavior" ("Little Children," *Ensign*, Nov. 1986, 16). Knowledge truly is power.

CHAPTER 6
SERVING WITH HONOR—
HAVING NO REGRETS

Every day can be a great day on your mission. Missionary work is an expression of conversion to Christ due to the love of God and Christ in our lives. It has been said that, "The natural expression of the love of God is sharing the gospel with your fellowmen." This statement expresses the total mission of Christ and the Church in preaching the gospel, redeeming the dead, and perfecting the Saints. We do the work of Christ by expressing His love and by serving mankind—those in the Church and those who haven't yet found it, those on the earth and in the spirit world—with our stewardships given and assigned through the priesthood of God. We are responsible and accountable to carry the gospel to every nation.

Missionaries must understand and appreciate the following: Without vision, the people perish. Realizing a vision requires organization and planning, and without it we remain overwhelmed, frustrated, and find ourselves complaining against the "system," thinking others don't understand. The absence of vision often occurs due to lack of training, and to misunderstanding responsibility and accountability.

Too many missionaries spend a great deal of their mission trying to adjust or learn the necessary skills for teaching the gospel. These missionaries do great when they learn, but now the Lord has raised the bar. We need to be ready to hit the ground running when we enter the field. The Lord doesn't want to hear His missionaries say, "If only I had known this before. . . ." He wants them to get to work and progress beyond what we now imagine.

Being rooted in Christ and expressing your testimony of this through actions and words should be the goal of all those preparing for serving missions. In this chapter, and a few following it, we will discuss what we can learn now—socially, emotionally, and spiritually—to be great missionaries.

PLANNING

How do you begin to have a great day? You have to plan. You've heard the old cliché, "If you fail to plan, you plan to fail." Another way of putting it is, "Organize yourselves, prepare every needful thing" (see D&C 88:119). If you do not plan well, it is very difficult to have a good day. Too often we just put out brush fires because we fail to make an overall plan. The principle of planning is eternal. The principle of organizing is eternal. Joseph Smith taught that, in Genesis, the verb for describing the creation of the earth, the Hebrew word *Barau*, means "to organize" (*The Words of Joseph Smith: The Contemporary Accounts of the Nauvoo Discourses of the Prophet Joseph,* eds. Andrew F. Ehat and Lyndon W. Cook [Provo: BYU Religious Studies Center, 1980], 397). So organizing means creating. You can "create" a wonderful mission and a wonderful life.

Create a great day by planning. Have a vision of what you want to be, and how you plan to accomplish that. Do you have a vision of what you should radiate? Have you made a mission statement about what kind of missionary you're going to be? Do you have a plan as a missionary to find souls every day? Every moment of every day is a finding moment. Do you have a plan to teach with power by the Spirit? Do you have a plan to help your investigators progress by making and keeping commitments? Do you have a plan to help keep them active? Do you have a plan to help the less active? Do you have a plan to not only place copies of the Book of Mormon, but get promises to read them? Do you have a plan to serve your companions? There are missionaries who are like that. There are missionaries who care because they have the love of God and they make a plan that shows they care.

If you do not plan, the river of life will just take you any way it's going. And so will your mission. Whatever is happening, you'll just follow the flow. You need a plan. Plan to always show love. On your mission, four hours a week are designated to give service, Christian service, to go out and do something to help somebody else. That's part of the plan. Isn't that interesting? The prophet says that missionaries in the full-time service of the Lord should be sure to take four hours a week and give unsolicited Christian service. Oh, I love the prophet. He reveals truth to us, and everything we receive from him is literally a plan from God.

Be a planner. Be administratively sound so you can be spiritually in tune. I like that. If your apartment is dirty, and your clothes are hanging all over the place, and there are pots in the sink and your clothes aren't ready for the day . . . then you just kind of feel yucky and that means you're not administratively sound. If everything is in its place, you'll be surprised how easy it is to be spiritually in tune. Organize yourself, then you will never be rushing around inefficiently, for you are prepared for the day. The Gods had a purpose and a cause. They had power, material, and direction. They created the eternal plan and put in place mankind so we could prove ourselves. Priesthood on earth has a purpose and a cause—so that we could proclaim the gospel and perfect and redeem mankind. This very earth is the result of a plan.

We often lightly treat the command to ponder, plan, and organize every needful thing. We say, "I don't have time to plan and organize." Then we have frustration, chaos, and fail in our stewardship. To plan is the beginning and necessary step in missionary work. This way every day will be a great day on your mission.

As you plan and prepare, it is important to set your goals. They need to be smart goals. In *Leadership for Saints*, Rodger Dean Duncan and I present a major point concerning SMART goals.

> The whole point of setting goals, of course, is to *achieve* them. The best goals are *smart* goals. Actually, *SMART* goals is more like it. SMART stands for the five characteristics of well-designed goals.
>
> *Specific:* Goals must be clear. Vague ambitions and platitudes have no place in goal setting. When goals are specific, they tell people precisely what is expected, when, and how much. Only with specific goals are you able to measure progress.
>
> *Measurable:* What good is a goal if you can't measure progress? When goals are not measurable you never know if or when or even how you're making progress toward their completion. Not only

that, but it's very difficult for people to stay motivated to complete the goals in the absence of milestones to indicate progress.

Attainable: Goals must be realistic and attainable. As we indicated earlier, goals should give people something to stretch for, but they should not be out of reach. Neither, of course, should goals be too easy. Goals that are set too high or too low become meaningless and people tend to ignore them.

Relevant: Goals must be an important element in the overall plan of achieving your mission and reaching your vision. It's estimated that 80% of people's productivity often comes from 20% of their activities. You can guess where the remaining 80% of effort ends up. Relevant goals address the 20% of the effort that has the greatest impact on performance.

Time-bound: Effective goals have starting points, fixed durations, and ending points. People are better able to focus their efforts on goal attainment when they are committed to deadlines. Goals without schedules or deadlines tend to get lost in the rush of day-to-day life.

(Roger Dean Duncan and Ed. J. Pinegar, *Leadership for Saints* [American Fork: Covenant Communications, 2002], 94–95.)

To begin this process we need to:

1. Understand the key governing principles in setting our goals and making our plans.
   - Vision—seeing your goals and your capacity to achieve them
   - Desire—being motivated to succeed
   - Preparation—being willing to pay the price
   - Enthusiasm—being inspired of God
   - Commitment—desiring to make and keep covenants
2. Set your goals—short term, intermediate, and long range.
3. Make your plans to achieve your goals.
4. Act upon the plan.
5. Measure and report on your efforts.
6. Evaluate your entire effort as it relates to your key governing principles of success . . . and then *begin again.*

It is this "beginning again" after you've set and accomplished goals that makes the difference. Ever working, ever improving—this is what it means to serve with all your heart, might, mind, and strength.

Use of Time

Live a worthwhile life. Make every second count. "Behold, this life is the time for men to prepare to meet God; yea, behold the day of this life is the day for men to perform their labors" (Alma 34:32). We truly should work as if every day was our last. The following illustrates the precious commodity called time.

Each Day Is a New Account

If you had a bank that credited your account each morning with $86,000 . . .

That carried over no balance from day to day . . .

Allowed you to keep no cash in your account . . .

And every evening cancelled whatever part of the amount you had failed to use during the day . . .

What would you do?

Draw out every cent every day, of course, and use it to your advantage.

Well, you have such a bank . . . and its name is
"TIME."

Every morning, it credits you with 86,400 seconds.

Every night, it rules off as lost whatever of this you have failed to invest to a good purpose.

It carries over no balances.

It allows no overdrafts.

Each day, it opens a new account with you.

If you fail to use the day's deposits, the loss is yours.

There is no going back.

There is no drawing against the "Tomorrow."

It is up to each of us to invest this precious fund of hours, minutes, and seconds in order to get from it the utmost in job performances and personal happiness.

How many minutes do you have each week to use effectively to bring to pass the eternal life and immortality of man?
—Anonymous

BE SINGLE-MINDED

The first thing to remember is that we came to this earth to do the will of our Father. In the premortal councils we agreed we would come and do our best to return to God's presence by doing His will. To accomplish this, we cannot have one foot in the world and one foot in the kingdom. It is impossible. Our eyes must be single to the glory of our Father.

We must leave our cares in the hands of our Heavenly Father (see D&C 100:1–2). If our eye is single to His glory, our whole body will be filled with light, and the light is the Lord Jesus Christ (see D&C 88:67). That's what gives us power. If we ever, ever lose the desire to do the will of the Father, we will have a very difficult time on our mission. Like Nephi of old, He will prepare a way for us to accomplish the things He commands us to do (see 1 Ne. 3:7). Ammon knew where his strength came from: "I know that I am nothing, . . . [but] in his strength I can do all things" (see Alma 26:12). Yes, if we agree to do the will of the Father, keeping an eye single to His glory, our Father will strengthen us and provide a way for us to accomplish our righteous desires.

No Regrets—Hard Work and Diligence Are the Keys

President Benson, when speaking to the mission presidents, mentioned that 95% of all the problems in the missionary field could be solved with work. Work, work, work, that's the key to success. Idleness is the den of iniquity, and every time, every single time, an elder has a problem in the mission field, it is because he's idle. Idleness can and will destroy. When you grow up and have children, be sure to have them work. Just have them work. Keep them busy. I never realized how important that was until I was older. I'm thankful for my father because he taught me to work and obey. The work ethic is crucial on a mission.

One time I was out to dinner with my sweetheart, and an elder there said, "President Pinegar, our mission was right next to your mission. You know, I couldn't understand why you were having so much success there."

And I said, "Well it wasn't me, it was the missionaries and the Lord; I just happened to be there."

He said, "Well yes, but I was talking to one of your missionaries the other day and told him I couldn't understand why I wasn't more successful. And then he told me about the work ethic of your mission. And you know what? We didn't work as hard as your missionaries did."

I said, "I understand. I would actually have to say, 'Elders, please don't get up so early. Be sure to be in bed on time because you're all working too hard.'" Can you imagine the joy of that for a mission president? I actually heard the missionaries say, "President, I have the greatest schedule. I'm up at 4:30 now, I've exercised by 5:30, I've got everything done and we're out at 7:30, instead of 9:30, and I'm getting in about seventy-five hours a week." I'd look at them and just hearing them talk I'd get tired. But they were so devoted, and you know what happened? I watched on a regular basis as missionaries' bodies were renewed. The sisters, they were magnificent. The young elders, they were magnificent. The couples, oh they were just wonderful. The older single sisters were just beautiful. I can't tell you how much I loved them because I knew they were working for the Lord, and working together. It was sheer joy.

Your work ethic must be beyond reproach, but working hard is not enough. You must work smart. You must organize your time so that when you work you're effective in your work. Don't arrive in one area, then go to another, then another, in the same day. Plan your work to be in one area so you save all that travel time. Organize your time to work hard and smart. It helps you to have a happy day.

Reports with a Purpose

Recognize that your reports are numbers that reflect your Christlike service and that they lead to baptisms. Everything you do leads people to Christ. Do not separate numbers from people or do not look beyond the mark, for you came to bless people's lives by accepting Christ through the ordinance of baptism.

Attitude

Having a positive attitude toward life, the Lord's work, and yourself is very important. It sets the stage for every day of your life. Satan's outlook is negative, and he seeks to make you miserable, as he is (see 2 Ne. 2:18). The Lord's outlook is positive, and he seeks to fill you with joy (see Mosiah 4:20). Recognize and remember the goodness of God, count your many blessings, and look to bless others—these things will help you have a positive attitude and stay focused on the work.

Remember, now that you are here make your mission the best. You have the power to choose and to act rather than to react. You can make the difference. Every area is terrific. Bloom where you are planted. Your success is not the result of your environment. Never blame anyone for anything. Simply go forward, doing your best in the strength of the Lord, and you will be happy.

One day a missionary asked, "President Pinegar, why are you always so happy and positive?" I replied, "I'm my Heavenly Father's boy." That simple fact has helped me all my life. We are all God's children. We are of great worth. We have the capacity to be like our Father. If you remember these things your self-respect will increase. You will choose to serve and bless others, fulfilling your divine role as a child of God.

Prayer

Plan to pray. Pray with all your heart, might, mind, and soul for direction, for strength, for courage, for your investigators, and for people to love and to serve. It's a key to a great day. Prayer is so powerful that all of the great gifts of God—revelations, faith, humility, charity, and so many more—come as a result of prayer. Remember James 1:5, "If any of you lack wisdom, let him ask of God." Joseph Smith asked Heavenly Father, and what was the result? The First Vision. Lehi received the vision to leave Jerusalem when he asked Heavenly Father. Doctrine and Covenants section 138, that glorious vision about the redemption of all who have died without a knowledge of the gospel, was a result of Joseph F. Smith asking about the scriptures. Joseph Smith, reading the Gospel of John, asked Heavenly Father about the resurrection of souls. The result was Doctrine and Covenants 76. If we don't ask in prayer, we take away one of the greatest blessings of our lives—revelation and direction from our Heavenly Father.

I'll never forget a conversation I had with my colleague, Truman Madsen, as I was coming out of my Book of Mormon class. I looked at him and said, "Tru, what is the greatest need in the Church today?" And I just wondered what he would say, because he's so wonderful and kind and sweet and brilliant and bald, and all those wonderful things. And he said, "Ed," and he took about one second, and finished, "prayer." You think about prayer. Without it we cannot have charity.

You want to have a great day on your mission? Be full of love: "Pray unto the Father with all the energy of heart, that ye may be filled with [His] love" (Moro. 7:48). When fast Sunday comes around next month, what are we going to do? We're going to pray and fast for charity, for faith, and for our investigators. Fast and pray for things that will make you a better instrument in the hands of the Lord.

Be Humble

What about our humility? Humility is being totally dependent upon God and developing a relationship with Him. The fruits of humility are being submissive, meek, lowly, patient, and teachable. These are the qualities that help us realize we're totally dependent upon God; and at that point we can begin to have a relationship with Him. Prayer is the expression of our humility. For example, when we say, "Heavenly Father," we've acknowledged our relationship—child and parent. When we say, "We ask Thee," we show our dependence upon Him. Isn't that wonderful? Humility is personified through our prayers, and as we pray we will be full of humility and faith. An example of this is found in the Book of Mormon: "They did fast and pray oft, and did wax stronger and stronger in their humility, and firmer and firmer in [their] faith" (Hel. 3:35).

Temptation and Obedience

When it comes to the adversary, we must have a plan. Satan is attacking more forcefully than ever before. Prayer helps us resist temptation. As missionaries, we've got to avoid temptation: "Watch and pray always lest ye are tempted" (see 3 Ne. 18:15–18). To have a great day on your mission, you must overcome temptation.

One of the best ways to stay out of temptation's path is through active obedience. The angel came to Adam and said, "Why dost thou offer sacrifices unto the Lord? And Adam said unto him: I know not, save the Lord commanded me" (Moses 5:6). Total, complete loyalty and obedience to your mission president and other leaders is like unto being obedient to your Heavenly Father, for it is the law. When His righteous servants speak, it's the same as if the Lord speaks (see D&C 1:38).

Never set aside mission rules, supposing you know better yourself, for that is a tool of the devil. Never think that a little rule doesn't matter, for that is how the flaxen cord works (see 2 Ne. 26:22). When you become at peace in obeying the rules, you will become at peace with yourself and with your Heavenly Father. Remember, if you follow the Lord's servants you follow Christ. Any time you resent mission rules, you will find yourself with a poor attitude. You will backbite, you will complain, and you will find fault, and in so doing you will separate yourself from the Spirit of the Lord, no longer able to receive revelation. Always sustain your leaders. Those that support and sustain their leaders always do better. Remember, sustaining the prophet means you also sustain all the people under him in the priesthood line, and then you will have the blessings of the Lord.

If you ever set yourself up as the judge, the jury, and the maker of the rules, then you will not be happy. You will not follow the counsel the Lord has given you through the proper channels of authority, and you'll wonder why things are not going right. So, to have a great day on your mission and in life, do as your mission president asks, and you shall be blessed. And remember, when you are busy obeying, you don't have time to entertain temptation.

Avoid Contention

Contention in and out of the mission field—backbiting and gossiping—probably ruins more days than anything else. We must learn to bridle our tongue and our passion; to speak kind and loving things, and to avoid contention. Contention is of the devil (see 3 Ne. 11:28–29).

Yes, to have a great day, we do our best and the Spirit will guide and direct us. Then we'll have no regrets. I heard Bishop Hales speak at the MTC once, and he said, "Return with Honor." So then I encouraged my missionaries to "Return with honor with no regrets." The main thing is to do your best. Sometimes, at the MTC, the elders might not have been at their perfect best. People would say,

"President Pinegar, do you know what the elders did?" And I would say, "Do you mean some of the Lord's anointed weren't perfect yesterday?" And they kind of bowed their heads and walked out the door because they'd realized that sometimes we're not at our best. Forgiveness then became the watchword. And all of a sudden, doing our best was doing our best to forgive and to forget and to move forward. Yes, the days will be hard. You might say, "How can you say it was so good when it was so hard?" Every day can be fulfilling.

If you are going to have a great day on your mission, you've got to remember the words of Mormon to his son Moroni: "Notwithstanding their hardness [the investigators or the difficult situations], let us labor diligently; for if we should cease to labor, we should be brought under condemnation; for we have a labor to perform whilst in this tabernacle of clay, that we may conquer the enemy of all righteousness, and rest our souls in the kingdom of God" (Moro. 9:6).

Service

Seek to serve. Once you start thinking of yourself, that's when the problems begin. Your problems will become difficult when you become selfish in nature rather than looking to serve. So, every morning say, "Whom can I bless? Can I call anybody up to help them?" In other words, a seeking-to-serve attitude makes a difference on your mission.

One of the biggest problems in the mission field is the use of numbers. Everyone says, "Oh, my zone leader, all he cares about is my numbers. Six first discussions. Five copies of the Book of Mormon. Two committed. Five second discussions, four other general discussions. All they do is call me up and say, 'What are your numbers?' And I feel like I'm just a machine out here turning in numbers." And the only reason missionaries feel that way is because they don't understand what a number means. In the field, when you think of a number, think of the number of people you are blessing. For example: "Dear President, this week was a joyful week. I had the blessing of teaching six special people, children of God, the first discussion of the gospel of Jesus Christ. Oh, and several of them are going on with the second and third, and we've had some of those already. It was wonderful, President. It's so good. Yes, six discussions."

People often separate the number from what the number stands for. Numbers in the mission field are a representation of your Christlike service to Heavenly Father's children. "Heavenly Father, today's a great day. I taught six of Thy children the first discussion. I placed two copies of the Book of Mormon with two people who promised to read it, and I feel so good." Numbers represent Christlike service, and you become validated by the Lord with each one you report. You should never seek to contend with your companion or your leaders because of numbers—just catch the vision.

Watch Over the Fold

If we read the great commandment in Matthew 22:36–40, we find that love is the fulfillment of all the law and the prophets; because in the love of God, and the love of Christ, all things are fulfilled. Now you can understand why love is the key to the entire plan of salvation.

When Jesus was talking with His disciples at the Sea of Tiberias, He said, "[Peter], lovest thou me?" And Peter answered, "Yea, Lord, thou knowest that I love thee" (see John 21:15). In the Greek New Testament, the word "love," the first time it occurs when used in the Aramaic or Hebrew, translates into three forms. These three forms of "love" English just does not describe. In Greek they are *agape*, which means unconditional love; *philia*, which means brotherly and reciprocating love; and *eros*, which means physical love.

So the Lord says to Peter, "Peter, agape me?"

And Peter says, "Yea, Lord philia."

Then the Savior tells Peter to feed His sheep. The Lord then asks again, "Peter, agape me?"

To which Peter answers, "Yea, Lord, philia."

Finally, the third time, the Lord gives up and He says, "Philia me, Peter?"

"Yea, Lord, philia."

Then the Lord instructs Peter, "Feed my sheep." And what the Lord was maybe trying to say was, "Peter, do you love as God loves? Can you be unconditionally kind? Can you *act* rather than *react*? Can you avoid being vindictive, and look to be prayerful and be kind? Can you avoid contention? Can you seek the Spirit? Can you find something to praise, rather than find fault?"

Unconditional godlike love means that you have ultimate concern for every person you see in this world, and that brings about righteous service. Now think about that as it relates to Christ—ultimate concern. God loves His children. Jesus Christ loves His brothers and sisters, Heavenly Father's children. He has ultimate concern for our welfare; He died on the cross and suffered for our sins in Gethsemane that we might live again and be resurrected, if we would but repent. That's the kind of ultimate concern that brings about righteous service.

Unconditional godlike love means that I love you, and I separate you from your behavior. No matter what you do I will always love you and try to help you come unto Christ. The point is this: look for the good, look to serve, and look to be a beacon of light rather than a judge.

To be a great missionary, you must look to serve like Christ did. You must have His ultimate, twenty-four-hours-a-day concern. You must be a full-time minister, a full-time servant, every day. You're not just to baptize and forget them. You're to be out there every day, building up the kingdom of God, strengthening members and building confidence with them. Visit those who are less active. In our mission we had a goal to visit one less-active member every day. Within six months two hundred members were reactivated and four hundred more had come to church, just because our missionaries were seeing less-actives as well. You don't put notches on your belt when you baptize. You don't put hash marks in your journal. No, no, no! You put the name of the child of God you were able to serve.

Self-Esteem

Remember, you are to serve the Lord. Keep your mind focused on the Lord's work. You have the power to bless people's lives. This will make the ultimate difference in your attitude and self-image. You are the Lord's anointed servant to do His will, to bless people's lives. Whom the Lord calls, the Lord qualifies. Recognize your powers and potential. Remember, the Lord expects you to become like Him—a step at a time. You are divine in your nature. Never forget that.

I love Abinadi. To me, Abinadi was the epitome of the great missionary because he practiced the doctrine of doing the will of the Father. As you recall the story, King Noah was leading his people astray. Abinadi was sent there to preach and they tried to kill him, but he said (I'm paraphrasing here), "It mattereth not what you do to me and my body, but I will do the will of the Father. I have come to preach the word, and after that, do whatever you will" (see Mosiah 13:3–9). They burned Abinadi at the stake. He was a martyr. His validation clearly wasn't a name-brand clothing label or any other temporal thing. His validation came from the Father because he did the Father's will. We probably won't be asked to die for the kingdom, but we are asked to live for it.

The only validation that matters is our Heavenly Father's approval of what we have done. Doing the will of the Father is the first great step toward having a great day, for He will validate us and give us strength, and we will feel good. If our mind is not single to His glory, and if we have our own agenda, we are in trouble whether we're a missionary or not, because our own agenda dictates our behavior. That's why we pray to Heavenly Father to direct our paths. We sing the primary song, "Lead me, guide me, walk beside me." The word of God is our director. The word of God is a representation of Christ. Yes, everything ties in to being single-minded. Once that is entrenched, every day will become a great day.

KEEP A SENSE OF HUMOR

It's okay to laugh. Keep a sense of humor so that things won't get too tough. A cheerful and light-hearted attitude goes a long way toward making a mission, and life, more enjoyable. Cheerfulness and a sense of humor are some of the most uplifting and contagious attributes one can possess. They brighten both the giver and those who choose to receive it. They give hope for the day ahead and even enhance physiological and emotional health. Cheerfulness and good humor come from seeing that we are all in the same boat. Laugh at yourself and laugh with others. Be cheerful despite life's adversities—it's a welcome commandment of God (see Matt. 9:3), and it makes life flow more smoothly. The psalmist said, "Serve the Lord with gladness" (Ps. 100:2). Make the decision to be cheerful. Make it a point to keep a sense of humor. Why are some people so spontaneously cheerful? Because they *choose* to be. And so can you.

REVIEW YOUR GOALS

Set achievable, measurable, and realistic goals and work toward them. And if you ever fall short of them, think positively, "Look how high I came because of the goal I set," rather than, "I failed." No one fails when they are doing the Lord's work.

The way to become a goal-achieving missionary is by keeping your mind focused on the reasons you are serving, and on how to become like the Savior. You can become a happy, successful, fulfilled missionary. The following list is a short summary of skills and attributes you should seek after if you want to serve a mission free of regrets. You can review it and your related goals every week.

Spiritual Skills and Attributes to Attain

1. Increase your desire to serve the Lord.
2. Gain empathy and understanding of your fellowmen.
3. Learn to love, and express love for your companion.
4. Develop a Christlike love for mankind, even as the sons of Mosiah did.
5. Improve in personal righteousness. Your level of obedience is directly proportional to your love of God.
6. Pray mightily.
7. Find, teach, commit by the Spirit. Yea, in all things be directed by the Spirit as a missionary.
8. Bear testimony continually to your companion and to every person you teach. As you bear it, the Spirit will deepen your testimony.
9. Develop tolerance and patience for all people in all stations of life.
10. Submit yourself to the will of the Lord. Humble yourself, be teachable and easily entreated that you might go forward, always praising the Lord, and being obedient to your priesthood leaders.
11. Gain confidence in teaching the word of God with love and by the power of the Spirit.
12. Increase your knowledge and skills of using the scriptures in all your discussions.
13. Gain a level of confidence in your communication skills. This comes with practice and with time.

14. Learn personal relationship skills with people. Learn to get along, learn to love, learn to empathize, learn to communicate one with another and be able to receive feedback.
15. Wax strong in boldness.
16. Learn to work with groups of people—with families, Sunday School classes, etc. Working with groups within the ward is vital, as member groups will increase your power to work with Heavenly Father's children.
17. Never, never contend about doctrine or religion or argue in general.

If you daily remind yourself of and continually apply these seventeen principles on your mission, you will become the kind of missionary that the Lord expects you to be, the kind described in "Marks of a Man."

Marks of a Man

As I jumped on board my flight from Miami to Salt Lake City, I paused a moment to catch my breath. Seated near the front of the plane was an excited young man, probably 19, sitting with his parents. His hair was short and his clothes new and sharp. His suit was fitted perfectly, and his black shoes still retained that store-bought shine. His body was in good shape, his face clear, and his hands clean. In his eyes I could see a nervous look, and his movements were that of an actor on opening night.

He was obviously flying to Utah to become a missionary for the Mormon Church. I smiled as I walked by and took pride in belonging to this same Church where these young men and women voluntarily serve the Savior for two years. With this special feeling, I continued to the back where my seat was located.

As I sat in my seat, I looked to the right, and to my surprise saw another missionary sleeping in the window seat. His hair was also short, but that was the only similarity between the two. This one was obviously returning home, and I could tell at a glance what type of missionary he had been.

The fact that he was already asleep told me a lot. His entire body seemed to let out a big sigh. It looked as if this was the first time in two years he had even slept, and I wouldn't be surprised if it was.

As I looked at his face, I could see the heavy bags under his eyes, the chapped lips, and the scarred and sunburned face caused by the fierce Florida sun.

His suit was tattered and worn. A few of the seams were coming apart, and I noticed that there were a couple of tears that had been handsewn with a very sloppy stitch.

I saw the nametag, crooked, scratched and bearing the name of the Church he represented, the engraving of which was almost all worn away. I saw the knee of his pants, worn and white, the result of many hours of humble prayer. A tear came to my eye as I saw the things that really told me what kind of missionary he had been. I saw the marks that made this boy a man.

His feet—the two that had carried him from house to house—now lay swollen and tired. They were covered by a pair of worn-out shoes. Many of the large scrapes and gouges had been filled in by the countless number of polishings.

His books—laying across his lap—were his scriptures, the word of God. Once new, these books which testify of Jesus Christ and His mission, were now torn, bent, and ragged from use.

His hands—those big, strong hands which had been used to bless and teach—were now scarred and cut from knocking at doors.

Those were indeed the marks of that man. And as I looked at him, I saw the marks of another man, the Savior, as he was hanging on the cross for the sins of the world.

His feet—those that had once carried Him throughout the land during His ministry—were now nailed to the cross.

His side now pierced with a spear, sealing His gospel, His testimony, with His life.

His hands—the hands that had been used to ordain His servants and bless the sick—were also scarred with the nails that were pounded to hang Him on the cross.

Those were the marks of that great man.

As my mind returned to the missionary, my whole body seemed to swell with pride and joy, because I knew, by looking at him, that he had served his Master well.

My joy was so great. I felt like running to the front of the plane, grabbing that new, young missionary, and bringing him back to see what he could become, what he could do.

But would he see the things that I saw, could anyone see the things I saw? Or would he just see the outward appearance of that mighty elder, tired and worn out, almost dead.

As we landed, I reached over and tapped him to wake him up. As he awoke, it seemed like new life was entering his body. His whole frame just seemed to fill as he stood up, tall and proud. As he turned his face towards mine, I saw a light about his face that I had never seen before. I looked into his eyes. Those eyes. I will never forget those eyes. They were the eyes of a prophet, a leader, a follower, and a servant. They were the eyes of the Savior. No words were spoken. No words were needed.

As we unloaded, I stepped aside to let him go first. I watched as he walked, slow but steady, tired but strong. I followed him and found myself walking the way that he did.

When I came through the doors, I saw this young man in the arms of his parents, and I couldn't hold it in any longer. With tears streaming down my face, I watched these loving parents greet their son who had been away for a short time. And I wondered if our parents in heaven would greet us the same way. Will they wrap their arms around us and welcome us home from our journey on earth? I believe they will. I just hope that I can be worthy enough to receive such praise, as I'm sure this missionary will. I said a silent prayer, thanking the Lord for missionaries like this young man. I don't think I will ever forget the joy and happiness he brought me that day.

—Anonymous

CONCLUSION

A happy, successful, and fulfilled missionary can be identified by the following traits:

1. They know who they are (see Rom. 8:16).
2. They know their calling is from God through His prophet (see 3 Ne. 5:13).
3. They are rooted to Christ and have a testimony of the Atonement (see Hel. 5:12).

4. They know the gospel, for they have searched the scriptures diligently, and they know the Church is true (see Alma 17:2).
5. They love their fellowmen (see John 13:34–35).
6. They feel confident in the strength of the Lord. They know the scriptures and live by the Spirit (see Alma 26:11–12; 2 Ne. 32:3–5).
7. They love the Lord and their mission leaders and show that love by obedience (see John 14:15).
8. They open their mouths and testify (see D&C 38:8–11). They know that the elect will hear the word of God (see D&C 29:7).
9. They feel the Spirit and they know that the Spirit is the power of conversion (see D&C 50:17–22).
10. They work with all their heart, might, mind, and strength. They work hard and are diligent in all things (see D&C 4:2).
11. They always remember that all their blessings are from God, and they exhibit an attitude of gratitude (see D&C 59:21).

CHAPTER 7
BEING A DILIGENT MISSIONARY

When I worked on the Church Missionary Training Committee, my assignment was to train mission presidents prior to their going to the mission field. In preparation for that training, I surveyed mission presidents already out on assignment and asked them what their main responsibility was. "Motivating missionaries is ninety-five percent of my work," they almost always replied. "Missionaries get discouraged, they get tired, they get worn out." One of the most difficult things we face as missionaries is staying motivated. This seems to be the challenge throughout every mission in all the world, and throughout life. Missionaries have good days and struggling days. We have successes and trials. Sometimes in our work we lose the power that is within us because we lose the vision, or fail to appreciate the Atonement and look to Christ for our strength. We can be continually motivated and successful missionaries if our perception is clear and our motives pure. Following up from the previous chapter, we will now take a look at another aspect of serving honorably. In loving the work, staying enthusiastic, working diligently and realizing our divine potential, we will have the motivation to continue, and no regrets for our lack of perseverance. We will be motivated by our love of God and our Savior Jesus Christ and concern for our fellowmen.

ENJOYING THE WORK

There are many reasons why we do what we do as missionaries. Most of the time there are a variety of reasons all acting at once. We grow and progress spiritually as our motives change. Sometimes missionaries would say to me, "I came just because all my brothers went; what else could I do? They would think I'd done something wrong if I didn't come."

I would say, "I'm just grateful that you're here, and I love you and I know the Lord loves you." Those same elders, weeks, or months, or maybe even a year later, would be in an interview and I would notice a glowing countenance. I would ask, "How do you feel about your mission now?"

And I would hear, "Oh President, I love the Jones family so much, I'm just praying that they'll come back into the Church," or, "I love the Brown family; I think they're ready to be committed to be baptized. Oh, I just pray that the Lord will be pleased with what I'm doing. I just want to do what He would have me do if He were here." Motives change because our relationship to Christ, and our understanding and appreciation of the doctrines, principles, and covenants of the gospel, have caused a change within us so that we do things for the right reasons, rather than just because we're told to do them.

Sometimes we are motivated by love, duty, responsibility, peer or parental pressure, even a desire for self-improvement, or self-esteem. Still, other sources of motivation come from our need or desire for success, respect, the love and trust of our leaders, a new value system, and joy. We can also be motivated by the vision of possibilities, and traditions of righteousness. And there is merit in all these motives. But our Heavenly Father, our Savior Jesus Christ, and the Holy Ghost are the supreme sources of motivation. The plan of our Heavenly Father, when understood, should give us all we need. If we are rooted in Jesus Christ, listening to the living prophets and adhering to the scriptures, we will have a continual, living well of motivation. We love God and our fellowmen, and *that's* why we do what we do.

It has been said that no one motivates us; rather, we are given information that we act upon, then we choose to be motivated. We can choose to be motivated when we understand the significance of the following questions: (1) Do we know our purpose? (2) Why are we truly here? (3) Do we recognize the worth of souls? (4) Do we understand the purpose of the Church? (5) Do we want all of our brothers and sisters to have a chance for happiness and exaltation? (6) And above all, do we comprehend the significance of the Atonement of Jesus Christ?

Many of the personal attributes we have already discussed will help us stay motivated as well: desire from within; the vision of the work; humility, which allows us to learn and submit to the will of our Father; positive attitude, which gives us hope so we're willing to press forward and work with all our heart; and being able to make and keep commitments and live a disciplined life. These attributes of success can help us stay motivated in the Lord's work.

We must also have increased desire to serve the Lord. How do we get this desire? When our faith increases, our love increases. We can understand our purpose. When we realize that we've been forgiven of our sins, we can taste the joy of the Lord. Alma, after his conversion, says that his joy was to preach the word (see Alma 36:24). He wanted everyone to taste of the joy he had tasted. Do you think Alma's desire was strong? Of course it was. Whenever we have any success, our desire will increase proportionately.

How do we keep our vision strong and the purpose of the work in our minds and hearts? It's when we realize the purpose of God's plan, and God's plan for us as missionaries. We become instruments through which Heavenly Father and Jesus Christ's purposes are fulfilled. We can do all things the Lord has asked us to do because we are His disciples. We are like Mormon when he said, "Behold, I am a disciple of Jesus Christ . . . I have been called of him to declare his word . . . that [people] might have everlasting life" (3 Ne. 5:13). In other words, when we catch the vision and understand His purposes, our motivation increases.

When we are easily entreated, it's easier to stay motivated. If we are always asking, "How come we have to do ten of those and five of these? Why are we working so hard? Why are zone meetings on this day instead of that day? Why are we doing this? . . ." then we are not easy to entreat. If we choose to always backbite and complain, we will not be easily entreated, and we will not stay motivated. Humility is the answer.

If you're rooted to Christ, you can stay motivated. When another door slams, you'll say, "Great, let the door slam. That will really give me a blessing, you know. Throw water on me, anything. I need the blessings." And if you have that kind of positive attitude, you'll be marvelous.

AN ATTITUDE OF ENTHUSIASM

Maintaining a positive attitude is the magic key to motivation. You can be no better than your attitude, because attitude is part of your perception. Perception comes through your past experience, your values, and your attitude.

I recall the story I once told to a group of people about a little girl in the fifth grade. It is picture day at school and she is so excited. Her mother says, "Let's put on your white dress; it's such a beautiful March spring day. The snow is almost melted. You will look so pretty in your white dress for the school picture." Once she is dressed in her finery, the little girl runs up quickly to the bus stop and she's first in line. Along comes a car, and splot, splat—mud all over her dress. Oh, it was horrible. She runs back home crying, "Mommy, Mommy, my dress is ruined, my dress is ruined."

Then she goes in the house and her mother says, "Well, let's put on your second-best dress." So she puts on her second-best dress and she runs back to the bus stop. Just as she gets to the bus stop she reaches up to grab the bus handle, but the bus driver didn't see her and he inadvertently closes the door, which hits her right on the nose—boom. Hemoglobin everywhere. She takes her little hanky and tries to stop her nosebleed.

She finally gets to school. She has a scabby nose, but she has her second-best dress on, so it's not too bad of a day. Well, she goes to morning recess on the north side of the building. There are a few little parcels of snow still left, and some boys in the fifth grade are making snowballs. They decide to throw one, and, lo and behold, it hits her right in the eye—kaboom! Her eye begins to swell up.

Next recess, in the afternoon, she climbs up on the tricky bars (the monkey bars today)—all the way to the top. There she is sitting at the top when she sees her friend Sally. She goes to wave and loses her grip and—khkh khkh khkh—falls all the way down and lands on her elbow. She screams, but as she screams, she notices something shiny on the ground and clutches it in her hand. She cries her way into the teacher and says, "My arm hurts." The teacher thinks, "Oh dear, it's probably broken." Then the school nurse comes and agrees that the arm is probably broken. "Let's put it in a sling and call her mother so she can take her to the doctor." So, they put the arm in the sling and her mother comes to pick her up. And there's her daughter: swollen eye, scabby nose, second-best dress on, sling on her arm, and a smile on her face. And she says, "Sweetheart, how can you smile on a day like this?"

And the little girl says, "Oh, Mommy, I found a nickel—it was my lucky day." Now that's what I call a positive attitude.

There are going to be days you get all the doors slammed, but to stay motivated, your attitude must be positive. Remember the Savior's admonition: "Blessed are all they who are persecuted for my name's sake" (3 Ne. 12:10). So every time we're persecuted, we're getting a blessing. That's the kind of attitude we have to have. It doesn't matter where we are; that positive attitude can save lives, because if we always feel good about ourselves and the work, then we'll keep plugging along.

In our mission we had an attitude of "always one more door." So we would knock on all the doors and one more. Well, one day we were having a zone meeting and one of the sisters stood up to speak. The sister said, "Oh, President, it was a hard day. It was raining and we'd forgotten our brollies [that's umbrellas in England]. Things weren't going well, and all I could remember you saying was 'one more door, one more door.' We were now sopping wet and you know what? I could just hear that little voice of yours, President, saying 'one more door, one more door.' I felt so good inside, and I kept saying, 'I've got a good attitude and I'm sopping wet, and I don't care.' And then we knocked on that one more door and this lady looked at us like, 'You poor little wet things, you'll turn into a fish if you stay out much longer.' And sure enough she invited us in and we gave a first discussion."

You must recognize the purpose of opposition in all things. It's here to stay. You must needs be tempted to know the good from the evil. You have opposition so you can grow, and you have the right to choose. You have moral agency, which is a gift from God. You can decide when you wake up in the morning if it's going to be a great day or not. Realize that you have the power to choose to react or to act. When we draw on the powers of heaven, and strengthen our spirituality through prayer and study and personal righteousness, we will gain confidence and our attitude will be positive.

And don't forget goal-making as a good way to stay motivated. Make reachable, measurable goals, with logical and systematic plans. Implement the plans by the Spirit with dates of accomplishment to do your work. And when you do that, you'll start to have a little more success. Success begets success, and then you'll *want* to keep working hard.

REALIZING AND REMEMBERING YOUR DIVINE POTENTIAL

If I could talk to you like you were just sitting right next to me, one on one, I would tell you that you are fulfillment of prophecy. As in Jacob 5:70–71, you are the one who is pruning the vineyard for the last time. You are among those of whom the Lord spoke in the Doctrine and Covenants 138:53–57. He talks about the temple and proclaiming the gospel to the vineyard again. Yes, you are one of the noble and great ones saved for this day. Do you realize how special you are? When you do, you will keep working. Realize that because of your exceeding good works in the premortal existence, you are now here, doing that great work of bringing souls unto Christ by building up the kingdom of God (see Alma 13:3–7). So I praise you; I honor you. You are held in high esteem. You must be instructed in the ways of the Lord, and then remember that you can do it. There's nothing you cannot do.

The Lord motivates us. We trust Him and we love Him, and He blesses our lives. He motivates us because we recognize our weaknesses and imperfections and trust Him to give us the help we need. He motivates us by showing us our divine potential, saying in effect, "You are my sons, you are my daughters, you can come and be with me." He motivates us by giving us the plan of exaltation, the plan of happiness. And, He motivates us by requiring us to make and keep commitments that He calls covenants—covenants that help us reach that potential. As your commitment to your covenants deepens, your motivation increases. We promised to help others (see Mosiah 18:8–9). Remember that God has covenanted with us to give us all things. Is this not motivation enough: exaltation and happiness?

CONCLUSION

We can be motivated in all things, but the key comes down to this: how converted are we to Christ and His gospel? How deep is our gratitude for His atoning sacrifice? Then we can be like the missionary who stood up and said, "It's the least I could do to be a good missionary after all my Savior has done for me."

Bringing souls to Christ is the goal and the reward. Nothing could make us happier. A missionary I taught in missionary preparation class just wrote me. He's serving in Germany. He wrote, "Oh, Brother Ed, it's so great. A sister is committed for February 8 to be baptized. It's like you said, I've never been so happy." And then he said some beautiful words, "I am continually being strengthened by the Atonement of the Lord Jesus Christ. There are elders and sisters who understand why we do what we do. And when we think of a baptismal goal, or any other worthy goals, it's because we love Heavenly Father's children." Surely this love will be our motive in missionary work. Love is the motive for Heavenly Father and our Savior in all that they do (see John 3:16; 2 Ne. 26:24), and it is our ultimate goal to be like them.

CHAPTER 8
OPEN YOUR MOUTH—
COMMUNICATING WITH LOVE

One of the most important things we have to do as missionaries is to open our mouths. There is no other way we can find Heavenly Father's children. We must prepare now to gain the knowledge and ability, then, when the time comes, the Spirit of the Lord will give us the words we need to say. Our duty as missionaries is to invite all people to come unto Christ; everyone has a right to come unto Christ.

The scriptures remind us that the harvest is ready and we are to gather it by means of opening our mouths. "Yea, verily, verily, I say unto you, that the field is white already to harvest; wherefore, thrust in your sickles, and reap with all your might, mind, and strength. Open your mouths and they shall be filled, and you shall become even as Nephi of old, who journeyed from Jerusalem in the wilderness. Yea, open your mouths and spare not, and you shall be laden with sheaves upon your backs, for lo, I am with you" (D&C 33:7–9). "Sheaves" means convert baptisms. When you open your mouths, you'll bring people to Christ. "Yea, open your mouths and they shall be filled, saying: Repent, repent, and prepare ye the way of the Lord, and make his paths straight; for the kingdom of heaven is at hand; Yea, repent and be baptized, every one of you, for a remission of your sins; yea, be baptized even by water, and then the baptism of fire and of the Holy Ghost" (D&C 33:10–11).

Because many are "kept from the truth because they know not where to find it" (D&C 123:12), our job is to overcome our fears so we can help people find the gospel. As missionaries and members, we are to find those who want to hear the word of the Lord; we made commitments at baptism that we would stand as witnesses of God at all times, and in all places, and in all things (see Mosiah 18:8–9). It is our duty. The two aspects I would like to cover are: (1) the art and skill of effective communication, and (2) having the courage to proclaim the gospel.

COMMUNICATION

The art of communicating requires the Christlike attributes of patience, understanding, empathy, being easily entreated, selflessness, integrity, humility, having a positive attitude, having respect, and many others.

Many skills can be acquired that will improve our communication: (1) Listening—with real desire to understand; (2) Realizing you could have misunderstood, misinterpreted, and even misheard the comment; (3) Attempting to state your comment clearly and ensuring the listener understands it the way you meant it.

My dear friend, Stephen Covey, has taught:

> When another person speaks, we're usually "listening" at one of four levels. We may be ignoring another person, not really listening at all. We may practice pretending. "Yeah. Un-huh. Right." We may practice selective listening, hearing only certain parts of the conversation. We often do this when we're listening to the constant chatter of a preschool child. Or we may even practice attentive listening, paying attention and focusing energy on the words that are being said. But very few of us ever practice the fourth level, the highest form of listening, empathic listening.

> When I say empathic listening, I am not referring to the techniques of "active" listening or "reflective" listening, which basically involve mimicking what another person says. That kind of listening is skill-based, truncated from character and relationships, and often insults those "listened" to in such a way. It is also essentially autobiographical. If you practice those techniques, you may not project your autobiography in the actual interaction, but your motive in listening is autobiographical. You listen with reflective skills, but you listen with intent to reply, to control, to manipulate.

> When I say empathic listening, I mean listening with intent to understand. I mean seeking first to understand, to really understand. . . . Empathic (from

empathy) listening gets inside another person's frame of reference. You look out through it, you see the world the way they see the world, you understand their paradigm, you understand how they feel.

Empathy is not sympathy. Sympathy is a form of agreement, a form of judgment. And it is sometimes the more appropriate emotion and response. But people often feed on sympathy. It makes them dependent. The essence of empathic listening is not that you agree with someone; it's that you fully, deeply, understand that person, emotionally as well as intellectually.

Empathic listening involves much more than registering, reflecting, or even understanding the words that are said. . . . In empathic listening, you listen with your eyes and with your heart. You listen (observe) for feeling, for meaning. You listen for behavior. You use your right brain as well as your left. You sense, you intuit, you feel.

(Stephen R. Covey, *The 7 Habits of Highly Effective People,*
[New York; Simon and Schuster, 1989], 240–41.)

Until we learn to communicate, no one will know our hearts, no one will know the love we have for them, and no one will know us. Communication is the key to building relationships of trust. A strong relationship is vital to both the receiving and giving of the blessings of the gospel.

Communicating with God

To communicate with others, we must first learn to communicate with the Father who gave us life; learning to communicate with our Heavenly Father becomes the foundation for all our communication.

We usually call this communication prayer; we might even say *mighty* prayer. In John the Beloved's Gospel he said, "And this is life eternal, that they might know thee the only true God, and Jesus Christ, whom thou hast sent" (John 17:3). Knowing God is an essential element of communication. The Prophet Joseph Smith said that before you can have faith in God, you must know Him and know His character (see *Lectures on Faith* 4:1). Those of you who have had the privilege of reading the *Lectures on Faith* know whereof

I speak, for the first lecture is all about the character and nature of God. Now that's interesting, because if you look closely at your first discussion, you will see it teaches that God is our Father, that He knows all, and that He is all loving and all powerful. It is about knowing God; and the main reason to know God is so we can be in tune with Him—usually through communication with Him.

Knowing Our Father

In section 67 of the Doctrine and Covenants, the Prophet received a revelation in Hyrum, Ohio, about knowing God. Verse 10 is especially beautiful because it relates specifically to missionaries:

> And again, verily I say unto you that it is your privilege, and a promise I give unto you that have been ordained unto this ministry, that inasmuch as you strip yourselves from jealousies [which are very bad] and fears [which are not very good], and humble yourselves before me, for ye are not sufficiently humble, the veil shall be rent and you shall see me and know that I am—not with the carnal neither natural mind, but with the spiritual.

In other words, we can never know our Father until we overcome jealousies and fears, and humble ourselves. We will discuss overcoming fears later in this chapter. For now, let's look at overcoming jealousy and obtaining humility.

1. Overcome Jealousy with Love. What would you say is the absolute antithesis, or opposite, of jealousy? It is love and charity, because jealousy cannot coexist with those feelings. If you find yourself feeling jealous of other people's intellect, their looks, their clothes, or their possessions, you know that in your heart you lack the love of God, and the love of Christ—even charity. It will be like a barometer. When you see somebody doing something good or doing something better than you, maybe looking better or wearing a nicer suit, you say, "Isn't that nice! Isn't that beautiful! Boy, he did well on that, didn't he!" Just watch yourself grow. You see, in the hereafter nobody is going to ask you what car you drove, or how big your house was, or what kind of hair you had (or, in my case, didn't have).

Look for opportunities to praise people rather than tear them down. When you tear others down, you go down with them. You dig your own pit. When you build people up, you rise with them. Jealousy can be destroyed through the power of love. This love comes from God, and as we develop it, we come to know Him and can better communicate with Him. We are better able to feel His love and convey that to others in our communications.

2. Learn Humility. Another step in coming to know our Father is humility. Until we humble ourselves, there will be no spiritual growth. It's interesting to note that in Helaman 3:35, the Nephites did fast and pray oft, waxing stronger and stronger in their humility. Isn't that remarkable? They grew stronger in what the world would call a weakness. That is because they drew nearer to God, and so became more like Him. If you want to be strong in humility, pray with real intent, and you'll have that humility. By exercising humility, love, faith, and knowledge—combined with mighty prayer—we will learn to know our Father.

Communicating with Others

There are three major areas to work on when communicating with others: expressing your love, building trust, and using the words of the Spirit. Building on the last concept we discussed, we also learn that the love of God helps us better communicate with others.

1. Express Your Love. We must understand that everybody really wants to be loved, and the people who seem the most cocky are often the ones who are most in need of love. Take the time to get down on the root level with others and show love.

I had some glorious experiences with the youth in our stake when we went on a pioneer trek. We divided up into "families." There was simply no one else for us to talk to but each other. All of a sudden we were all forced to learn the process of communicating.

After three days in the wilderness, a testimony meeting was held. I'll never forget one boy who thought he was pretty cool. He stood up and said, "I was with old Jason in our ward. I always thought that Jason was such a nerd, I wouldn't have given him the time of day. But let me tell you, Jason was in our family on this trek, and I got to know him, and now I love Jason. He is my dear pal, and we'll be friends forever. Oh, I love that guy! I wish I had taken the time before this to become his pal."

You can save yourselves a lot of problems during this earth life by expressing the love of God and the love of Christ through communication. Whether it be verbal, by touch, or by whatever means, please communicate your love (see John 13:34–35). I know it takes time and it takes effort, but nothing else you do during your mission will bring greater rewards. And without communicating your love, true communication simply won't occur.

Of course you won't meet people and immediately say, "Oh, you're great, and I love you!" That doesn't happen. Neither does "Oh, we're married in the temple. Great! That's it for eternal life—super!" It's like the man who said to his wife, when she was feeling unloved and unappreciated, "I told you that I loved you and that if it ever changed I'd let you know. So why are you so upset?" We all need more than that. Even I need to be told every day that I'm loved. When my daughter Tricia was a young girl she'd wait for me to get home every night. When I'd come in the door she would greet me with, "Hi, Daddy, I love ya!" My heart warmed, I smiled, and my burdens were lifted. In your communication, start the process now of working with yourself and with others and learning to express your love for others and the great work that you are doing.

2. Build Trust. In communication, one of the most difficult things to deal with is when we are doing something that may not be perfect, and we need counsel on it, and everyone else can see it except us. Let me tell you how it started in our family.

"Sweetheart," my wife said to me one day, "I think we need to take time to evaluate each other and how we're doing." So, we had our first big evaluation (we call it companionship inventory).

We sat down and I said, "Honey, how are you doing? How am I doing? What could I work on?"

"Oh, you're fine, sweetheart," she answered. "But it might be nice if you'd work a little more in the yard."

"What do you mean?" I bristled. *I've been slaving in mouths (I'm a dentist), filling cavities, taking out wisdom teeth—foraging in the field for food—and you're worried about whether or not I'm working in the yard!?* I didn't say that, but I thought that!

I simply wasn't ready to accept any constructive criticism. Feedback requires a person to say, "Tell me what I can change; I am ready and open and willing to listen." It almost takes the courage of David because our hearts are so very sensitive and vulnerable. What you have to do is establish trust in your relationship first. Once you build a relationship of trust, then you can communicate and say, "Help me." And when you do that, you will really begin to grow.

My wife can tell me anything now, and I'm so grateful because we have a relationship in which I can simply say, "Sweetheart . . ." and she understands what I'm trying to communicate.

The other day I was having a tough day, feeling a little sick and weak and powerless. I came into the house, found my darling wife, and said, "Sweetheart . . ." I was totally exhausted and I wanted to go to sleep, yet I knew I couldn't. She saw that, heard the plea in my voice, and gave me a hug.

"Honey, I just need some strength," I said. "I'm getting weak." I felt her strength in that hug pouring into me, sustaining me, and carrying me through the rest of the day. She understood my troubles, and loved and supported me with the love of Christ. She didn't say, "Why don't you do this?" or "Why don't you do that?" She didn't find fault with me or scold my weakness. She simply loved me because we share a deep trust in our relationship.

We will never be able to give or receive productive feedback until we build a relationship of trust. After we have reached that level, then we can be open and candid, and say, "Help me, Elder, or Sister, what do I really need?"

It's so wonderful now when my wife says, "Sweetheart, it would really help if you would . . ." And I can answer, "Oh honey, thank you, I'll be so much better." Being willing to accept feedback is a product of humility.

After we have a relationship of trust in our communication, we have enough humility to say, "okay, tell me because I want to grow." If we have an insatiable desire to be like the Savior, people can say,

"Hey, you've got to change that, you need to shape up." And we'll be able to answer, "Okay, okay, I'll be better." As missionaries, when you can do that, you will change for the better.

3. Use the Spirit's Words, Not the World's. We can only communicate honestly if we are led by the Spirit—in other words, when we ask ourselves in every situation, "What would Jesus do?" and "How would the Spirit direct us?" If any of you were to say "President, I need to see you" and then come in for an interview, long before you ever walked in the door, I would have already prayed: "Father, what wouldst Thou have me say by the Spirit if Thou wert here at this very moment?"

If our communication is honest and open, it will always be led by the Spirit, and that is vital in preventing hurt feelings. Communication should never be intended to harm anyone. Yet, so often our communication is flippant, light-minded, casual, and worldly. It seems that everything now has to be fun or funny. I'm not saying we can't laugh (I love to laugh as much as anyone else), but there's a right time and a right place.

Sober-mindedness is one of the most essential traits in order to be a spiritual giant, in order to speak by the Spirit, to be led by the Spirit, to be Ammon-like and Moroni-like missionaries. The language we use is an important key in maintaining sober-mindedness. Words like "He's a cool dude" are totally inappropriate when talking about spiritual things. Using sarcasm and phrases like "Hey, what a studman" are also totally inappropriate. That's the way the world talks, not the way the Lord would have His missionaries talk. We need to communicate the way the Spirit communicates—with love, tenderness, and sensitivity, as well as appropriateness. When we don't communicate properly we often offend and hurt others.

Do you know what it means when the scriptures tell us to say "yea, yea" and "nay, nay" (see Matt. 5:37)? It means that our integrity is so strong, that whatever we say is the final word on the matter and people can absolutely trust us. When we say yes, people will know that the answer is yes, and we won't have to take an oath. Our communication needs to be totally honest, straightforward, and on a higher plane than the rest of the world because we are disciples of Christ.

4. The Love of the Father Helps Us Communicate. When we communicate with our Father, we know how He feels, and through that communication, we also discover how we should feel. If you were to describe Heavenly Father's greatest feeling, what would it be? Love. That's the great motive in His eternal plan. And how is that feeling manifest? Where does it fit in the grand plan our Father has outlined? In His love for His children. John 3:16 describes the great love our Heavenly Father and the Savior have for us: "For God so loved the world, that he gave his only begotten Son, that whosoever believeth in him should not perish, but have everlasting life."

In other words, when you truly love, you empathize and feel for other people. The love that God the Father, Elohim, gave to us was His Son. Christ's love for us is explained clearly in 2 Nephi 26:24, "He doeth not anything save it be for the benefit of the world; for he loveth the world, even that he layeth down his own life that he may draw all men unto him. Wherefore, he commandeth none that they shall not partake of his salvation." He gave His life for us; He atoned. So love, then, should emulate this feeling, this empathy toward one another.

Now that we understand communication with the Father, we're moving to the next level. When we seek first to understand, then we will be more easily understood. When we understand, we can more easily empathize. Empathy simply means feeling how other people feel. When we empathize, we know we are communicating. If we haven't done that yet, then we haven't communicated, and we may just have a verbal barrage going back and forth. Remember, seek first to understand, then to be understood, and finally to feel how others feel. Then we will be communicating.

So, in communication we want to listen with our ears and our hearts so we can know and understand. Think of your own life when you've had a tough day. You felt misunderstood and unloved, didn't you? We've all had days like that. It really helps to have someone understand the way we feel. Communication, then, becomes a very important tool we can use on this earth to bring happiness—both to ourselves and to others. If we don't communicate our message, our message is not heard. You should be prepared to communicate.

5. The Spirit Is the Strongest Tool. After learning these keys to communication, the tool that will make all communication effective, both during your mission and in the future, is the help of the Spirit.

In Doctrine and Covenants 50, it states that the Spirit is a converter and a teacher; the Spirit is also a communicator. A great example of the power of the Spirit is recorded in 2 Nephi, "And now, I, Nephi, cannot write all the things which were taught among my people; neither am I mighty in writing, like unto speaking; for when a man speaketh by the power of the Holy Ghost the power of the Holy Ghost carrieth it unto the hearts of the children of men" (2 Ne. 33:1).

This is what can happen as we work on effective communication with the Spirit:

Neither take ye thought beforehand what ye shall say; but treasure up in your minds continually the words of life, and it shall be given you in the very hour that portion that shall be meted unto every man.

Therefore, let no man among you, for this commandment is unto all the faithful who are called of God in the Church unto the ministry, from this hour take purse or scrip, that goeth forth to proclaim this gospel of the kingdom.

Behold, I send you out to reprove the world of all their unrighteous deeds, and to teach them of a judgment which is to come.

And whoso receiveth you, there I will be also, for I will go before your face. I will be on your right hand and on your left, and my Spirit shall be in your hearts, and mine angels round about you, to bear you up.

(D&C 84:85–88.)

As we attempt to communicate, teach, and preach, the Spirit does most of the work (see D&C 100:5–6). Do you see why we pray for hearts to be softened? Do you understand why, when we're humble, we can communicate? The only way that we ever reach the point of getting down to the most basic level is when heart speaks to heart through and by the Spirit.

OPEN YOUR MOUTH

Now that we understand some important skills in communication, we must learn to put them to use. In his Epistle to the Romans, Paul proclaimed, "For I am not ashamed of the gospel of Christ: for it is the power of God unto salvation to every one that believeth" (1:16). We have nothing to be ashamed of in communicating the love of God to the world. We have no reason to fear, if we can but learn to open our mouths and share it.

I'll never forget when I served as a mission president in the MTC. The last meeting before the missionaries would go out, I would speak about being bold, obedient, full of love, and courageous in opening their mouths. "Do not be afraid. The worth of souls is great. You have a mighty role in the kingdom." Well, some of them were still afraid. I would ask them on their way to their mission to have an experience of opening their mouth. This sweet young sister wrote me a letter after she'd been out two weeks, and this is how it went:

Dear President,

After your talk Sunday night I was so nervous I didn't know what to do. I knew I'd be leaving Wednesday, and I was going to have to open my mouth. And I thought, *I can't do it, I can't do it.* So, I fasted and I prayed and I left Wednesday on the plane, and to my joy I had a window seat and my companion sat next to me. So I said, "Oh dear, I won't be able to talk to anybody on the plane," and I was so relieved.

But then, I got into the airport and I sat down, and here was a man sitting across from me. He was old and different looking, and I didn't know what to do. And all I could remember was your voice telling us, "Open your mouths, it will be filled, I promise you." Well, I girded up my loins and I opened my mouth and said, "Hi, where you headed?" From that little beginning we began an hour-long conversation. Pretty soon we became friends. And after a bit I said, "If you knew there was another book written about Jesus Christ, would you be interested in reading that? The Book of Mormon?"

He said, "Oh, I have a Book of Mormon." I committed him right there to read the book, and then he told me, "My daughter is taking the discussions too."

And then I said, "Is it okay if I have the missionaries come by and see you?" He said, "That will be just fine." Oh, President, it's so easy to open your mouth. The Lord will fill it. There's nothing to it.

I read that letter every time to departing missionaries because it helped them realize that we can all do it. All of us, member missionaries and full-time proselyting missionaries, can open our mouths and they will be filled.

Sometimes as missionaries, we are afraid to do our duty. We just can't seem to do it. Missionaries who had the hardest time in the mission field were the ones who were afraid, who were filled with doubt, and who thought they couldn't do it. So we have to learn how to overcome fear. Here are two more letters testifying to the ease of opening our mouths and overcoming fear if we simply have faith.

Dear President Pinegar,

On the way to L.A. from S.L.C., I was feeling a great deal of fear about opening my mouth. I wanted to share the gospel, but I was afraid of rejection. I sat down next to a man that, to be honest, looked very mean and unhappy. He was probably in his 70s and looked straight ahead without saying a word to me. It took me a good 10 minutes to muster up enough courage to say "Hi!" I did it because I remember the words you had said about "opening your mouth." You know, it really worked! This man needed someone to talk to. He just needed someone else to initiate the conversation. He told me all about himself and I told him about myself and why I was going to Korea on a mission. He was impressed. He had a daughter who was having the discussions and already owned a copy of the Book of Mormon. Well, by the end of the flight we were on a first-name basis and he said he would always remember that flight and me. I got his address and told him I would write him from Korea. I also committed him to read the Book of Mormon. On the flight from L.A. to Korea, our district gave out seven Books of Mormon and made about ten total contacts, with one commitment for a first discussion.

One of the elders was having a Korean gentleman who knew some English help him with his Korean. He then gave him the Book of Mormon and the man read it for about an hour on the plane ride.

Tell all those missionaries that if they fear, they doubt the power of God because although we are weak, if we have faith and open our mouths, He will fill them. He has the power to make us do incredible things—I've felt it!

Sister Rebecca Ivie
Korea Seoul Mission

Dear President Pinegar,

When I got here at Arcadia, I wasn't here half an hour before I was blessed with the opportunity of being persecuted for the Lord. Persecution is a lot easier to take when you think of it that way, then you aren't as likely to have contention in your heart. In fact, we had two people yell at us from a corner while we were on our bikes. We turned around, asked them what we had done to them to deserve such ridicule, and they couldn't think of anything. So we asked them what they knew about us, and why two normal-looking young men would be riding bikes in 80-degree weather in suits and ties. Well, to make it short, we gave out two copies of the Book of Mormon and made an appointment to teach them at a city park the next day. They came and brought a friend. While we were teaching, a group of boys between 14–16 came and, slowly but surely, they were drawn to what we were saying. We now have over

10 people that we are teaching just because we asked why they were yelling things at people they didn't know. Doesn't the Lord work in a mysterious way?

Elder Beck
California Arcadia Mission

Finally, before we move on to a practical discussion about steps we can take in overcoming our fears, I would like to share a poem that reminds us of *why* we should open our mouths, and how the Lord will help us do it. Reflect on this elder's testimony.

Open Thy Mouth
Try to remember the worth of a soul
I open my mouth and try to speak
But fear engulfed my breast
Takes over the flesh that is so weak

Deep within, a voice sounds so low
I love them, even as I love you
Be not afraid of what they shall say
And do not fear what they shall do.

For I have promised to guide your way
Sending you angels from on high
Just trust in me with all thine heart
And listen close for I am nigh.

Now open your mouth, I'll loose your tongue
And share what I have given to thee,
Thy brothers and sisters need thy help
Show them the truth and set them free.

Only by helping your brother's boat
Can you come unto the shore
So, bring them up and unto Me
And lo, you have come unto my door.

I open my mouth again to speak
With urgency my voice must ring,
The time is now, I cannot wait
I've been called to serve my King.

—Elder Ronald Clair Lowe
(Written while in the Provo MTC)

Five Ways to Overcome Fear

We overcome fear with faith, love, knowledge, preparation, and experience. Fear is a destroyer of faith. Our prayers cannot be with real intent when we are suffering from fear.

1. Faith in the Lord Jesus Christ. If you exercise faith and mentally exert that power, fear and doubt will flee away. The Apostles of old asked the Savior to increase their faith (see Luke 17:5). Faith comes by hearing the word of the Lord. Every time you read the scriptures, every time you hear your president speak, every time you talk together as companionships, or listen to your mom and dad, the word of the Lord will come into your heart and your faith will increase, and you'll become like Nephi and Lehi, the sons of Helaman, whose faith was so strong that they converted thousands of people (see Ether 12:14). Faith destroys doubt and fear, as shown in the scriptures: "They did fast and pray oft, and did wax stronger and stronger in their humility, and firmer and firmer in [their] faith" (Hel. 3:35). Faith is the first step toward decreasing your fear.

2. Love. Perfect love casteth out all fear (see 1 Jn. 4:18). Think about it. If you're full of love, then there's no room for fear. When love is in your heart, how you feel about the worth of souls is overwhelming. You will have such concern that you will do anything to help them come unto Christ—you won't fear doing a single thing. Such was the example of the sons of Mosiah in their concern for their fellowmen (see Mosiah 28:3).

3. Knowledge. Knowledge is power. When you see and understand, you know what's out there and you're never afraid. I remember when I was little, I'd say, "Can you leave the light on just a little bit?" And then I wouldn't be quite so afraid. But then one time when I was a little boy we saw a scary movie. It was something like *Frankenstein*

Meets the Werewolf with the Mummy. I know that sounds funny, I mean, now it would be a G-rated movie and we'd say, "Oh look how funny it is," but in those days, I was just a little nine-year-old boy, and I hid behind the seats. At that same time we lived on a farm. To irrigate our orchards, we would receive water from Strawberry Reservoir. The times when it was our turn to receive the irrigation water was called a "water turn." Well, on one occasion it came at midnight. Now, my duty as the youngest boy, the baby of the family, was to do whatever my big brothers said. So my job was to go down to the end of the furrow, and when the water got there, say, "The water's here," and that's all I had to do. But, you must understand, it was midnight and there was a full moon. I knew the werewolf was going to come. He was going to be there—there was no way out of it. I was frightened but I couldn't chicken out in front of my brothers. So, I started walking down the row, and the pheasants were flying by, and I thought, *Heavenly Father, I'm going to be a good boy. Don't let me die.* I was afraid. Why was I so afraid? Because I couldn't see. There was no light. I was afraid because of the past experience of that movie. When we don't have enough understanding, we don't trust in God and we fear what others will think or what may happen to us. When we gain enough knowledge, we see clearly, we have power, and then fear will flee from us. That's how knowledge overpowers fear.

    4. Preparation. When you're prepared, fear is overcome: "If ye are prepared ye shall not fear" (D&C 38:30). Preparation, like knowledge, is power. Self-confidence increases with our level of preparation.

    When vision and desire are in place, preparation becomes the master. It takes time, effort, dedication, and often sacrifice in order to prepare well. Make yourself fully capable of doing all that is required. Be sure you are spiritually, emotionally, and mentally prepared with every needful thing. The greatest act of preparation is to form an uncompromising vision of being successful at the objectives you have committed yourself to achieve.

    Make a detailed checklist of things you need to do in your preparation. What are the target goals, objectives, deadlines, and milestones? Select target dates along the way to be sure your preparation is on schedule. How will you know you have succeeded? By measuring and evaluating as you go. Make midcourse corrections as you go—preparation is an ongoing process. Preparation is more important than we sometimes realize. We must make preparation in all things a permanent part of our lives. We must organize well so that preparation and planning get adequate time to help us achieve our goals. With this aspect of our mission in place, we will feel more in control, fear will not be part of our lives, and we can expect greater success. Make a goal to prepare well, and then enjoy the blessings of success in your life.

5. *Experience.* The more you do a thing, the more your fear decreases. When new missionaries spent their first full day in our mission, the assistants to the president would teach them the dialogues and how to open their mouths. Then we'd send them out on the streets to meet people, just to open their mouths. The experience was something like this: "Would you be so kind and friendly as to answer a few questions that could bless your life? It'll only take a minute." That was the big number-one question, after which we asked questions about life, our Savior, families, the Book of Mormon, etc. But, it was just that simple: "Hi, would you be so kind and friendly as to answer a few questions?" And after one day the experience helped conquer their fear. When we recognize that we are instruments in God's hands, disciples of Jesus Christ and filled with love, we can open our mouths.

Obedience

It's kind of interesting how, when we understand the vision of the work, life changes. My dear friend Cyril Figuerres said these words: "Obedience is the price, faith is the power, love is the motive, the Spirit is the key, for Christ is the reason." When we know what Christ has done for us, we will want to open our mouths, and they will be filled with everything we need to say. The Lord will indeed bless us. The law of the harvest is there: "There is a law, irrevocably decreed in heaven before the foundations of this world, upon which all blessings are predicated—And when we obtain any blessing from God, it is by obedience to that law upon which it is predicated" (D&C 130:20–21). This law is to open our mouths, and they will be filled, and blessings will be ours.

The Lord has cautioned us, "But with some I am not well pleased, for they will not open their mouths, but they hide the talent which I have given unto them, because of the fear of man. Wo unto such, for mine anger is kindled against them. And it shall come to pass, if they are not more faithful unto me, it shall be taken away, even that which they have" (D&C 60:2–3). We must overcome our fears so that we can preach with power and find Heavenly Father's children. They too can then enjoy the gospel of Jesus Christ.

When we open our mouths, sometimes we don't know exactly what to say, so we need practice. In our mission there was a rule, you could not pass anyone on the street without saying, "Excuse me, would you be so kind and friendly as to answer a few questions?" And pretty soon, all the missionaries understood, and all of a sudden, baptisms weren't thirty a month, but they were one hundred thirty a month. Why? Because the Lord blessed the missionaries because they were obedient.

Here is one of the most beautiful parts of the process. If you've studied, if you've pleaded with the Lord, and if you're worthy and desire righteousness, you're being obedient. Then words and ideas will come out of your mouth that you've never even known.

The other day I was speaking to a group, and afterwards a man came up to me and said, "That was the most profound statement I've ever heard in my life."

"What was?" I asked.

"When you said that truth without testimony is hollow." He had it written down on a piece of paper.

"Wow," I said. "Who said that?"

"You did."

"When?" I asked.

"Just now, in that room."

"Can I write that down?" So I wrote it down, and now I'm sharing it with you. And why was I able to say that? Because the Lord inspires us; sometimes we don't even realize what we've said! In fact, I once heard President Marion G. Romney observe that he always knew when he had spoken by the Spirit because he learned from what he had said.

Even when we don't know exactly what to say, if the words we utter reflect the feelings of our hearts, the strength of our character, and the depth of our testimony, then the Lord will help us. President Monson promised us that whom the Lord calls, the Lord qualifies (Thomas S. Monson, *Live the Good Life* [Salt Lake City: Deseret Book, 1998], 121).

The Lord's Promise

I will never forget two sisters. It was a dark, dark night in the heart of London. So dark that they were anxious. A man came up by them at the bus stop, a large, dark man, and they were nervous. And then they said they remembered what President Pinegar said: "Don't fear, the Lord is before your face. He's on your right hand, he's on your left hand, His Spirit is in your heart, His angels round about you" (see D&C 84:88). So these two sister missionaries spoke. "Excuse me sir, would you be so kind and friendly as to answer a few questions that might bring you happiness?"

And he said, "Well, I'd be glad to, young ladies." And he did. He was from the Solomon Islands. He was in England for four weeks. He heard the message, and, since the sisters cannot teach a man alone, they went to the church to find others. Later this man, Peter Salaka, said, "I want to meet your president." So I went with them on a discussion. Peter Salaka is an elect man of God; just like we learn in the Doctrine and Covenants, that the elect shall hear his voice and know that it's true (see D&C 29:7). These two sisters taught him. We arranged for a baptism. Peter Salaka spoke at his own baptism. It was the greatest talk I have ever heard at a baptism. It was like he was a bishop already, like he'd been in the Church all of his life. I thought, *Who is this man?* They took him to church on Sunday, where he was interviewed and ordained to the office of a priest. He then left for the Solomon Islands, which was in one of the Australian missions at the time. I called the Australian mission president and informed him of the baptism of Peter Salaka, who lived in the Solomon Islands. He said, "That's great. That's part of our mission. I think we have one member there on that island. We'll see what we can do."

Time went by, and Elder Sonnenberg, of the Quorum of the Seventy, who was the president of the Australian area, and Elder Faust, then a member of the Twelve, went on a visit to the Solomon Islands to see what they could do to start the branches there. Peter Salaka greeted them at the airport. "I am Peter Salaka, and this is my son. I am a priest in The Church of Jesus Christ of Latter-day Saints. How can I help you build up the Church here?" Elder Sonnenberg sent me a picture of Elder Faust, himself, and Brother Salaka. Where would he be if those two magnificent sisters had not opened their mouths? If we allow one person to walk by and not open our mouth, we deprive them at that time of the opportunity of exaltation. This isn't a business; this is a matter of spiritual life and death. I am grateful that those faithful sisters opened their mouths so that they could be the instruments in the hands of the Lord to bless that great brother.

Make sure you open your mouth. Do not be afraid. You'll never know who will be a golden contact. You would never want to judge who that might be. But if you're dedicated, the Lord will help you find them. And if you're obedient, the Lord will remove your fears and gladden your heart and fill your mouth. "Therefore, dearly beloved brethren, Let us cheerfully do all things that lie in our power and then may we stand still, with the utmost assurance, to see the salvation of God, and for his arm to be revealed" (D&C 123:17).

CONCLUSION

Do you believe now? Do you believe that? Whenever you open your mouth it will be filled. It is so easy. Plead with the Lord to soften the hearts of the people so they will receive you. Exercise your faith. The Lord promised that He would go before you to prepare the hearts and minds of the people to accept the gospel. He will lead you to those that are prepared.

When we learn to love and care so much for our brothers and sisters that we'd do anything so that they might not endure endless torment, we will gladly pay the price to learn to communicate—with love, knowledge, and faith. Nevertheless, it can be tough. There will be times when you want to walk away, when you want to say, "I don't care." That's the biggest mistake of all! I hope you understand that as we grow in the gospel, as we gain a greater desire to show and give love, we can become great communicators by and through the Spirit. When the Spirit comes upon us, we will communicate appropriately.

I pray that we care enough to pay the price to communicate in love, thereby becoming great disciples of the Lord Jesus Christ. I know what we are doing is the Lord's will. I know it is important. I know the transcending events of our lives are when we communicate with people to bless them. I would hope that we would often get on our knees and pray to our Father to gain a testimony of these truths, and to gain His assistance in our communication efforts.

CHAPTER 9
TEACHING

As we progress through this book, we are trying to raise ourselves to the level the Lord expects us to achieve. Now that we have learned about how we should communicate and share the gospel, it is time to learn another aspect of our service to the Lord. We need to prepare ourselves as teachers.

Teaching is the greatest power on the earth to facilitate growth. Whether by precept or example, a skillful teacher has the power, by the Holy Spirit, to create an atmosphere of learning. The Spirit can inspire change—those we teach will want to repent. As missionaries and teachers of the gospel of Jesus Christ, we seek to do His will and teach His gospel by the power of the Holy Ghost. We are empowered by the Spirit as we live the gospel and prepare ourselves to be instruments in His hands.

LIKENING THE SCRIPTURES TO OUR LIVES
President Ezra Taft Benson taught us the following:

> We are to use the Book of Mormon as the basis for our teaching. The Lord states: "And again, the elders, priests and teachers of this church shall teach the principles of my gospel, which are . . . in the Book of Mormon, in the which is the fulness of the gospel" (D&C 42:12).
>
> As we read and teach, we are to liken the Book of Mormon scriptures unto us "that it might be for our profit and learning" (1 Nephi 19:23).
>
> (*The Teachings of Ezra Taft Benson*, 306.)

Here are some things the scriptures expound upon regarding teaching:

- "And also trust no one to be your teacher nor your minister, except he be a man of God, walking in his ways and keeping his commandments" (Mosiah 23:14).

As the scripture in Mosiah teaches us, we have responsibilities as teachers and learners that those who teach should truly seek to be worthy by keeping the commandments. Pray for those who teach to be worthy and prepared to teach by the Spirit.

- "And the Spirit shall be given unto you by the prayer of faith; and if ye receive not the Spirit ye shall not teach" (D&C 42:14).

We simply cannot teach without the Spirit. We should seek the Spirit for He will tell us the very things we need to say (see D&C 100:5–6). We will teach by the power and authority of God (see Alma 17:3). We will teach them to walk in the ways of the Lord and to love and serve one another (see Mosiah 4:15). We will teach by the Spirit of Truth and they will hear by that same Spirit (see D&C 50:17–22). These are some things we must remember as we teach the word of God.

HAVING AN EFFECTIVE TEACHING EXPERIENCE

Following is a list of seven qualities that make one a good teacher (missionaries are teachers of the highest order) and create an effective teaching experience:

1. A True Teacher Will Always Teach by the Spirit

We prepare for the Spirit by being obedient to the commandments (see D&C 20:77, 79), full of love (see D&C 76:116) and by exercising our faith (see 1 Ne. 17:10).

2. A Teacher Is Motivated by Love and Respect

The key ingredient is love. Above all other qualities, a teacher has a generous measure of love for the learner. Why would someone be devoted and committed to the growth and progress of another? Because of love. There is no other explanation. Your challenge is to love those you teach. Truly care for them so they know you care.

3. A Teacher Is Visionary

- *Focus on the potential.* A teacher sees less of what is, and more of what might be. Above all, a teacher has faith, confidence, and hope in the outcome of the teaching process, because only where the mentor sees clearly the potential of the student can that student be taught to catch the vision of his or her own future.
- *Open the eyes of your investigators.* A teacher illuminates new pathways. The key to change for investigators is to make sure they understand and appreciate the discussions and see their value. This improves their attitude and encourages a change in behavior—they will want to repent.
- *Illuminate the understanding.* If an investigator has had their eyes opened to new pathways, what does a teacher do but open up the vision of better ways to move forward on that path—to guide investigators toward better opportunities to seek growth and toward better knowledge for effective living and learning?

4. A Teacher Is Exemplary of the Learning Process

- *Know the doctrine.* Through your preparation you will gain confidence and demonstrate your credibility because you have paid the price to know the doctrine through hard work and dedication.
- *Know your investigators.* Know their needs, concerns, strengths, desires, etc.
- *Earn their trust.* Establish a relationship of trust and be trustworthy. Always be exemplary in all things.
- *Be humble.* A master teacher is humble, ever willing to confess that he or she likewise is a student who must continue to learn each day, to increase in the mastery of the doctrine of the gospel of Jesus Christ. All learning depends on an openness to learn, and on the courage to confess a need to learn and improve.

5. A Teacher Builds an Environment for Optimal Growth

- *Create a loving and learning atmosphere.* Create an appealing atmosphere for learning and change. This does not refer to the physical space as much as to the framework for learning—the vision, the relationships, the opportunities, the excitement, and the encouragement.

- *Focus on desire.* When you create the desire to learn, the biggest part of learning has occurred. In reality it is the investigator who makes the difference; they choose to accept or not. Desire is the fuel for learning.
- *Listen.* A master teacher listens. This skill nourishes the understanding and allows the teacher to discern the needs, prospects, potential, and strengths of the individual. Only through understanding can genuine teaching take place.
- *Master the techniques that foster learning.* Teach efficiently and effectively. When the heart is touched there is greater change.
- *Use action.* Involve them in the process. Discovery learning is very powerful.
- *Use high energy.* Make learning fun and exciting. It truly can be the adventure of life.
- *Encourage investigators to reach.* Help them stretch beyond their level. It inspires creativity and discovery.
- *Be gracious.* Never embarrass an investigator in front of anyone.
- *Use praise.* Praise your investigator for what they do.
- *Be creative.* A teacher is resourceful and innovative. No legitimate option for learning is left unattended and unapplied where it might assist the investigator to have the "aha" moment needed for true discovery.

6. A Teacher Has Endless Patience

- *Never give up.* A master teacher is patient. Some investigators grasp immediately; others take more time. What makes the difference in the outcome? Patience, longsuffering, gentleness, and nurturing. You cannot force a young tree to grow up any faster than nature has provided for its growth. Likewise everyone learns and grows at a different rate.

7. Have Relentlessly High Expectations

- Always expect the best of those you teach and treat them like they are the best. Remember that they are a divine child of Heavenly Father and have endless potential.

PREPARING OURSELVES TO BE POWERFUL TEACHERS

There are many steps we must take and things we must daily remember that will help us become the kind of teachers that the Spirit can work through. Some of them, and the blessings that come from them, will be discussed in the following sections.

Recognize Heavenly Father's Children and They will Recognize Themselves

I was at the hospital a few days ago, smiling at everyone I passed in the halls, when I realized that each one of them was one of Heavenly Father's children. Then I realized that there are more than five billion children of Heavenly Father on this earth, and that there have probably been that many before now, and for all I know, there may even be five billion yet to come. I wondered how righteous people should feel about Heavenly Father's children. Then I thought of Ammon and Omner and Himni and Aaron (they were righteous after they repented, as all of us become righteous after we repent) and how they felt about Heavenly Father's children.

In Mosiah 28:3, the sons of Mosiah had just talked to their father, King Mosiah, who was a very great man (his best friend was Alma the prophet, so he must have been a great man). They said, "Dad, could we please go to the Lamanites and preach?"

Those Nephites with minimum mentality probably wondered, "Why would you want to work with those savages who are trying to kill us?" But this is what the sons of Mosiah thought: "They were desirous that salvation should be declared to every creature, for they could not bear that any human soul should perish; yea, even the very thoughts that any soul should endure endless torment did cause them to quake and tremble" (Mosiah 28:3). They didn't see these Lamanites as enemies, but as fellow children of God who needed the gospel too. That's why they were such successful teachers of the word.

Now, if you apply the Atonement to your lives, then you'll taste His love and want that privilege for the investigators you teach. This is the most incredible thing you will ever see in conversion: when the power and love of God is placed in an anointed servant of God, and that servant teaches the worth of souls to those honest in heart. You can watch those people change before your very eyes. All of a sudden, their eyes will start to light up. They'll say, "Oh yes, I see, tell me more!" And in this process of enlightenment, guess what they receive? The gift of self-esteem. They recognize where they came from—"I am a child of God and I now understand His plan for me, and I want it. I want to be baptized."

Desire to Love Your Fellowmen that You May Teach Them

Did the sons of Mosiah have the love of God in their hearts? Did they have the love of Christ in their hearts? Even the very *thought* that any human soul would be in the telestial kingdom, or any place unsuitable for Heavenly Father's children, caused them to tremble and quake. Think of how you feel when someone you love is sick. You've all prayed for brothers and sisters, cousins or aunts, grandmas and grandpas, fathers and mothers, right? "Oh Father, please let them live! Oh, don't let them die!" We plead for mortality like it's the end of the earth.

If I were to run to you in a panic and say, "Come quick! Tricia Pinegar [my daughter] is lost up in the mountains. She's lost! My baby!" I wouldn't even doubt that you would come and help me. I know you'd come because you enjoy helping people who need help. It's interesting that we will pass by those who don't physically appear to need help, but we will quickly run to help others whose need is more obvious. However, there are some who are struggling with far greater danger and heartache. Until you love others and until you desire the welfare of their souls, you will never teach people with sufficient power to bring them to a knowledge of Christ. That is what I want to teach you: to preach and teach with power. So begin by desiring to love your fellowmen enough that you will be able to teach them with the Spirit, that you might bring souls to Christ.

The Power of the Spirit Carries the Message to Their Hearts

With that desire starting to kindle in our souls, we can do anything. If our investigators want to stop receiving the discussions, we'll say, "Oh please, won't you listen one more time?" They often won't listen until they see your true concern, but when they see and feel your concern for them, you will have the power to awaken their souls to God. You will have savor. Do you know what savor is? In

Doctrine and Covenants 101:39–40, we read: "When men [and women] are called unto mine everlasting gospel, and covenant with an everlasting covenant [and we've done that], they are accounted as the salt of the earth and the savor of men; They are called to be the savor of men; therefore, if that salt [you and I] of the earth lose its savor, behold, it is thenceforth good for nothing only to be cast out and trodden under the feet of men." In other words, to be "the salt of the earth" and "the savor of men" means to have the power to awaken people to God. But if we don't desire to do this, we'll lose our savor and never have this power and influence.

When you have the salt within you and the savor is in your soul, the Spirit will do its part. As Nephi explains, if you have this desire, despite your weaknesses, the power of the Spirit will carry it into the hearts of investigators and the less-active members you meet (see 2 Ne. 33:1).

The Lord Is in Charge

In 1 Nephi 4:6, Nephi said, "And I was led by the Spirit, not knowing beforehand the things which I should do." That didn't mean that Nephi hadn't studied or prayed or worked. He had already been righteous up to this point. But at that moment he didn't know what to do. You will probably have the same thing happen to you throughout life. You'll say, "Oh Father," and at that moment, when you ask what you should do, all of a sudden the words will come. You'll find yourself saying, "And by the power of the Spirit, I testify to you, Mr. Brown, that what I have said is true, and I know it's true because the Lord bore witness to me that it's true." You will bear your testimony with power, and then you'll wonder, *How did I do that?* Remember, the Lord is in charge! You can trust in Him.

When you teach with power, you teach the mind and the will of God. You fulfill Doctrine and Covenants 68:4; you speak by the Spirit, and the Spirit speaks the word of Christ, which is the mind and the will of God.

Obtain the Word

When you care enough for the people you're teaching, and you have the desire to do your best, the Lord will put into your heart and bring to your lips the things you should say at the very moment that you need them. When you have this desire, you are willing to pay the price to gain the knowledge to teach. Do you recall the Lord's words in Doctrine and Covenants 11? "First seek to obtain my word, and then shall your tongue be loosed" (v. 21). That's why you are here, to obtain the word. Then you will be given the power. If you just go out in the field and say, "Oh, Heavenly Father, I haven't searched the scriptures, I haven't learned my discussions, but I'm a nice guy and I'm out here, give me the words," then you'll find yourself saying, "I can't understand why that discussion didn't go very well."

Do you remember what was happening about the time of Alma 17:2–3? Alma had gone one way and the sons of Mosiah had gone another way, and they met up again as the sons of Mosiah were traveling toward the land of Zarahemla. Alma must have said something like, "Oh, Ammon, Omner, Himni, and Aaron, it's so good to see you," and no doubt they exchanged embraces. Then Alma said that what added to his joy was that his friends had "waxed strong in the knowledge of the truth" and that "they were men of a sound understanding." Why? Because "they had searched the scriptures diligently, that they might know the word of God."

For missionaries in the field, the hours between 7:30 and 9:30 in the morning are gospel study time and companion study time, when you role-play and study so you might also know the word of God. Many missionaries don't do that properly. Doctrine and Covenants 130:20 states that all blessings are predicated upon laws we must obey. When we study, we gain knowledge. If we don't study to obtain the knowledge, the Lord will not automatically give it to us and bring it to our memory in tough situations.

Don't Eat Your Spiritual Feast Intravenously

Have you ever pureed anything? That's where you take the Osterizer and chop something up at a very high speed. Have you ever pureed a filet mignon and then drunk it? Doesn't that sound stupid? Who in their right mind would take a filet mignon, medium rare, and say, "Well, it's time for a filet, great!" and toss it in the blender. You wouldn't do that! You'd take a knife and fork, and you'd slice the meat, and you'd put it in your mouth and begin to chew. You might even roll your eyes back, savoring that bite, and in your heart thank

Heavenly Father for food. (Ooh, I can taste it right now!) And you would chew it slowly so you could enjoy it. You would smile between each bite and each chew.

That's the way you need to read the scriptures. You don't speed through like you're on a bullet bike. You don't say, "Oh yeah, I read the Book of Mormon" while you're thoughtfully tapping your finger on your chin, trying to remember when that happened. You don't say, "Oh yeah, I took a speed-reading class and I can speed-read an entire chapter in five seconds." That's like getting food through intravenous feedings. You'd get just barely enough to stay alive!

Now, do you think Ammon, Omner, Himni, and Aaron were entitled to any more of the Spirit of the Lord than we are? You'd better not, because they weren't. They had to "search the scriptures diligently" (see Alma 17:2–3) just like we do. The biggest miracle in the world is conversion, and the missionaries who have this great converting power are the missionaries who pay the price. But if you set your study aside, supposing that you know of yourselves, or thinking that you can wing it or just take it easy, you'll be the missionary who says, "Why is this so hard? My momma didn't tell me it'd be like this. President, I want to go home. I'm not having any fun. Other missionaries told me this would be the happiest two years of my life, and I don't feel much happiness."

I'll tell you something. I certainly knew a lot of happy missionaries, because they worked and they studied as hard as they could. They were men and women of sound understanding, and they did wax strong in the knowledge of truth because they had gained this knowledge through diligent work and study.

This knowledge comes through searching the scriptures and good books. I had the joy and the privilege of teaching the Book of Mormon for a long time—about twenty-seven years. That's eight years more than most elders have been alive! I studied and I taught that book. Oh, how I love that book! Last December, I realized that my old scriptures were crinkled and the back was broken. So I decided that I needed some new scriptures and I bought two sets: a set that I carry around with me and a large set that sits on my desk.

I read the New Testament, the Book of Mormon, the Doctrine and Covenants, and Pearl of Great Price, and I marked all of these books. I didn't just read the books; I feasted upon the words, intensely searched them, and pondered them. Then I would underline and apply a particular scripture to my life. So when I read, I had to go slowly.

After that I went to my wife and said, "Sweetheart, I don't know what's wrong with me."

"What's the matter, honey?" she asked.

I answered, "I just finished the Book of Mormon again and it's like I read it for the first time."

She said, "What do you mean?"

I said, "I've never learned so much in my life!" So I prayed and I said, "Father, why? Why am I just learning this now? Why did I learn so much more this time than the last twenty-five times?"

And the answer was something like this: "My son, you were a good boy before and you're still okay, but you see, you read it this time with a different purpose in mind. The last time you read, you were just reading for a little knowledge for a class—like it's just part of the job, something you do because you have to. This time your mind isn't thinking of anything except how you can bless Heavenly Father's children. You are totally consumed with how you can use the book, how you can live the book, and how you can bless lives every minute."

Do you know the beautiful part about a mission? The only thing that you do is missionary work. You go to sleep and you wake up and you do missionary work. And elders and sisters (Hallelujah!) don't have to think about girls or boys or dates or ask, "What'll we do tonight, where shall we go?" You don't have to think about any of those things! All you do is eat, drink, and sleep the scriptures, pray and ponder, and ask how you can bless Heavenly Father's children so they'll come to Christ.

Here is a little parable for you. A rich young nobleman (let's call him Elder Milligan) walked up to Socrates and said, "Socrates, you are so smart." Socrates was a little embarrassed and blustered around a bit modestly, and Elder Milligan continued, "I would like you to teach me all that you know."

Socrates said, "You bet I will, I'll teach you. I'll give you all of my knowledge." He invited Elder Milligan down to the river, and they hiked down the path together. When they got to the river, they walked into the water until they were about up to their chests and old

Socrates said, "Look up there." The rich young nobleman looked up, and as he did so, Socrates (who was unusually strong) pushed him under the water and held him there. Elder Milligan tried to get up but Socrates wouldn't let him. As Elder Milligan struggled to break out of the old man's grip, he felt the air leak out of his lungs until there wasn't any air left. Just when he decided he was about to drown, Socrates let him up and said, "When you want to learn as badly as you wanted to breathe, you come back and I'll teach you all I know."

My point is, that until you have an insatiable desire to gain the knowledge you need, to know your discussions, to know how to find people, and to be able to build relationships of trust, you will never be able to teach with power. How does the Lord teach that same thing in the Beatitudes? He said, "Blessed are all they who do hunger and thirst after righteousness, for they shall be filled with the Holy Ghost" (3 Ne. 12:6). If you want to learn, if you care about these people, then pay the price to learn. Get that knowledge.

Purify Ourselves and Remember Who We Represent

So, we've got the desire and we have the knowledge, or we're working on the knowledge. Now we need to purify ourselves. Do you ever wonder why some missionaries can't do things that others can do? Why some people can perform miracles that other people can't? In 3 Nephi we read: "And there was not any man who could do a miracle in the name of Jesus save he were cleansed every whit from his iniquity" (8:1). Now, if you'd like to, cross-reference that to Doctrine and Covenants 76:69, which teaches us, "These are they who are just men made perfect." They are the ones who enter the celestial kingdom.

Do you want to be a just person and see miracles in your life? We read how in Moroni. We're told that angels ceased to come because the people lacked faith (see Moro. 7:23–30). If you have faith, what happens? You repent just like Enos did. He asked, "Why am I free of this guilt, Father?" And he was answered, "Because of thy *faith* in Christ, whom thou hast never before heard nor seen" (see Enos 1:8; emphasis added).

What is required of us in order to be cleansed from iniquity? Five thousand years of righteousness? No, just honest faith unto repentance. This is the key: if you do something wrong, repent. Don't muck in the mire, don't live in the past. Repent. You will also see how incredibly happy people are when they finally realize that they can repent, and you will watch the light come into their eyes because of what you've given them—the knowledge that they can repent.

When we repent in righteousness through confession and forsaking, and through good works, we become sanctified. We become holy and pure, without spot, so the Lord can work with us. That's why repentance is a daily ritual. Do you know what happens as we become purified? We become worthy instruments.

We learn about "worthy instruments" in Alma 29:9. Alma said, "I know that which the Lord hath commanded me [now remember to apply this scripture to yourself], and I glory in it. I do not glory of myself, but I glory in that which the Lord hath commanded me; yea, and this is my glory, that perhaps I may be an instrument in the hands of God to bring some soul to repentance; and this is my joy." Purity and purification make you an instrument in the hands of the Lord, and the Lord will use us if we desire it in our hearts and if we're trying to be purified.

You might say, "President Pinegar, that's the trouble! You quote from Alma here, and you quote from Enos there, and they're free from iniquity. You want me to be like them, and you forget who I am." No, that's the trouble. *You've* forgotten who you are. You are instruments in the Lord's hand just as any of the prophets are. All the missionaries of the Lord have power to call down angels. That's part of the power of faith which you elders and sisters have access to. Purify yourselves, and you will see miracles in your life.

Acquiring Faith

Now, let's think of some personal things we must do that involve our faith, our attributes, and our skills. First of all, you will teach with power no faster than you grow in faith, because faith is the foundation of all righteousness.

Many prophets and General Authorities have taught four ways to acquire faith. We can also increase our faith in other ways, but these are the primary ones: searching the scriptures, prayer and fasting, being righteous, and building up the kingdom.

Searching the Scriptures. President Benson said that searching the scriptures, the word of God, is the only way you can have faith. This is based on Romans 10:17: "So then faith cometh by hearing, and hearing by the word of God."

Prayer and Fasting. The second step President Benson taught is to acquire faith through fasting and prayer. Now think of Helaman 3:35 and Alma 17:3, where they waxed stronger in faith through fasting and prayer. Fasting + prayer = faith. When we fast and pray, we will also be filled with love, just as it says in Moroni 7:48. If we pray with all the energy of our hearts, we will be filled with the love of Christ, that we might preach the gospel and share it with our fellowmen.

Being Righteous. The third step is acquiring personal righteousness. Righteousness comes from obedience—and that will give you the Spirit. We covenant each week, as we partake of the sacrament, to keep the commandments by being obedient. The blessing associated with this is that the Lord promises that we can always have His Spirit to be with us (see D&C 20:77, 79). Faith is a gift of the Spirit (see 1 Cor. 12:9). We know that the gifts of the Spirit are predicated upon righteousness, and given to those who love God and keep the commandments (see D&C 46:9).

Building up the Kingdom. The fourth way to acquire faith is through building up the kingdom. You can be righteous by doing many things, but you are especially so when you're anxiously engaged in building up the kingdom. We not only acquire faith, but strengthen it by building up the kingdom of God. Faith is active whether we are hoping, working, or exercising its power. Therefore, as we seek to build up the kingdom by bringing souls to Christ, our faith increases. Just as bearing a testimony strengthens it, likewise, when we do faith-promoting things, our faith is increased (see Heb. 11; Alma 32; Ether 12; Moro. 7).

Faith is a multidimensional principle. Truly our faith increases with hearing the word of God, praying and fasting, living righteously, receiving the gifts of the Spirit, and building up the kingdom of God. Faith is enhanced throughout our lives. Whether we're looking at the creations of God, or seeing the good in mankind, we can increase our faith continually. And most importantly for our missions and lives, as our faith increases, we have the power to teach by the Spirit.

CONCLUSION

As you build and strengthen your faith, increase your love of Christ, wax strong in the knowledge of the truth, you will grow in confidence. You will be able to stand and give your first discussion with power and love. And if some of you forget something, don't worry. If you teach with love, people will understand. But you'll become so good once you have the Spirit that nothing can stop you. Those investigators and converts will call you blessed. And the day will come when Heavenly Father will thank you and say, "Well done, good and faithful servant; thou hast been faithful over a few things, I will make thee ruler over many things" (Matt. 25:23).

CHAPTER 10
THE SPIRIT

One recurring theme in preparation, living the gospel, and being missionaries is the key role of the Spirit. We must "raise the bar" in our own lives to become worthy of having the Spirit with us always. Think of what that means, having the gift of the Holy Ghost. We have the potential of the constant companionship of a member of the Godhead. The prophets and the scriptures have taught us clearly concerning the Holy Ghost and its importance in missionary work.

President Ezra Taft Benson counseled a group of newly called mission presidents: "Be guided by the Spirit. I have said so many times to my Brethren that the Spirit is the most important single element in this work. With the Spirit, and by magnifying your call, you can do miracles for the Lord in the mission field. Without the Spirit you will never succeed regardless of your talent and ability" (Mission Presidents' Seminar, 25 June 1986).

President Benson also said: "If there is one message I have repeated to my brethren of the Twelve it is that it's the Spirit that counts. It is the Spirit that matters. I do not know how often I have said this, but I never tire of saying it—it is the Spirit that matters most" (Mission Presidents' Seminar, 3 April 1985). Keep these ideas in mind as you ponder the following statements of prophets and apostles.

Joseph F. Smith said:

> The office of the Holy Ghost is to bear record of Christ, or to testify of him, and confirm the believer in the truth, by bringing

to his recollection things that have passed, and showing or revealing to the mind things present and to come. "But the Comforter, which is the Holy Ghost, whom the Father will send in my name, he shall teach you all things, and bring all things to your remembrance, whatsoever I have said unto you." "He will guide you into all truth." Thus, without the aid of the Holy Ghost no man can know the will of God, or that Jesus is the Christ—the Redeemer of the world—or that the course he pursues, the work he performs, or his faith, are acceptable to God, and such as will secure to him the gift of eternal life, the greatest of all gifts (John 14:26; 16:13).

(*Gospel Doctrine: Selections from the Sermons and Writings of Joseph F. Smith,* comp. John A. Widtsoe [Salt Lake City: Deseret Book, 1939], 101.)

James E. Talmage taught:

The office of the Holy Ghost in His ministrations among men is described in scripture. He is a teacher sent from the Father; and unto those who are entitled to His tuition he will reveal all things necessary for the soul's advancement. Through the influences of the Holy Spirit the powers of the human mind may be quickened and increased, so that things past may be brought to remembrance. He will serve as a guide in things divine unto all who will obey Him, enlightening every man, in the measure of his humility and obedience; unfolding the mysteries of God, as the knowledge thus revealed may effect greater spiritual growth; conveying knowledge from God to man; sanctifying those who have been cleansed through obedience to the requirements of the Gospel; manifesting all things; and bearing witness unto men concerning the existence and infallibility of the Father and the Son.

. . . The power of the Holy Ghost, then, is the spirit of prophecy and revelation; His office is that of enlightenment of the mind, quickening of the intellect, and sanctification of the soul.

(*The Articles of Faith,* 12th ed. [Salt Lake City: The Church of Jesus Christ of Latter-day Saints, 1924], 162–63.)

Brigham Young said, "The preacher needs the power of the Holy Ghost to deal out to each heart a word in due season, and the hearers need the Holy Ghost to bring forth the fruits of the preached word of God to his glory" (*Discourses of Brigham Young*, 333).

Wilford Woodruff explained that, "Unless you have the Holy Ghost with you when you go out to preach the Gospel, you cannot do your duty" (CR, Apr. 1898, 32).

Bruce R. McConkie expounded:

> True it is that honest truth seekers come to know the truth and divinity of the Lord's work by the power of the Holy Ghost: they receive a flash of revelation telling them that Jesus is the Lord, that Joseph Smith is his prophet, that the Book of Mormon is the mind and will and voice of the Lord, that the Church of Jesus Christ of Latter-day Saints is the only true and living Church upon the face of the whole earth. [Many] gain a testimony before baptism. But it is only after they pledge their all in the cause of Christ that they receive the gift of the Holy Ghost, which is the heavenly endowment of which Jesus spoke. Then they receive a fulfillment of the promise, "By the power of the Holy Ghost ye may know the truth of all things" (Moro. 10:5). Then they receive "the spirit of revelation, and the Lord tells them in their heart and in their mind whatsoever he will" (D&C 8:1–3).
>
> (*The Mortal Messiah: From Bethlehem to Calvary*, 4 vols. [Salt Lake City: Deseret Book, 1979-1981], 4:98–99.)

The scriptures teach us:

- "And now come, saith the Lord, by the Spirit, unto the elders of his church, and let us reason together, that ye may understand; Let us reason even as a man reasoneth one with another face to face. Now, when a man reasoneth he is understood of man, because he reasoneth as a man; even so will I, the Lord, reason with you that you may understand. Wherefore, I the Lord ask you this question—unto what were ye ordained? To preach my gospel by the Spirit, even the Comforter which was sent forth to teach the truth" (D&C 50:10–14).

- "Verily I say unto you, he that is ordained of me and sent forth to preach the word of truth by the Comforter, in the Spirit of truth, doth he preach it by the Spirit of truth or some other way? And if it be by some other way it is not of God. And again, he that receiveth the word of truth, doth he receive it by the Spirit of truth or some other way? If it be some other way it is not of God. Therefore, why is it that ye cannot understand and know, that he that receiveth the word by the Spirit of truth receiveth it as it is preached by the Spirit of truth? Wherefore, he that preacheth and he that receiveth, understand one another, and both are edified and rejoice together" (D&C 50:17–22).

- "And the Spirit shall be given unto you by the prayer of faith; and if ye receive not the Spirit ye shall not teach" (D&C 42:14).

- "And the spirit entered into me when he spake unto me, and set me upon my feet, that I heard him that spake unto me" (Ezek. 2:2).

- "And they said one to another, Did not our heart burn within us, while he talked with us by the way, and while he opened to us the scriptures?" (Luke 24:32).

- "And my speech and my preaching was not with enticing words of man's wisdom, but in demonstration of the Spirit and of power" (1 Cor. 2:4).

CONCLUSION

Let us never forget the role and function of the Holy Ghost. He is the key to teaching and righteous living.

- He shows a person what to do (see 2 Ne. 32:5; D&C 28:15; 39:6).
- He bestows the "fruits of the Spirit," which include such things as joy, love, peace, patience, and gentleness (see Gal. 5:22–23; Rom. 15:13; D&C 6:23; 11:12–13).
- He gives the "gifts" of the Spirit (see Moro. 10:8–17; D&C 46:11–26).
- He allows a person to speak with authority and boldness (see 1 Ne. 10:22; Alma 18:35; Moro. 8:16).
- He testifies to the truthfulness of God and other gospel principles (see John 15:26; D&C 21:9; 100:8).
- He helps us discern the thoughts or intents of others (see Alma 12:3; 18:16, 20, 32, 35; D&C 63:41).
- He gives us truth, knowledge, insights, understanding, and enlightenment (see John 16:13; 1 Cor. 2:9–11, 14; D&C 6:14; 11:13–14; 76:5–10, 116).
- He can bring ideas, concepts, or principles back to remembrance (see John 14:26).
- He can inspire a person in what to say in the very hour it is needed (see Luke 12:11–12; D&C 84:85; 100:5–6).
- He brings sanctification and remission of sins (see Alma 13:12; 2 Ne. 31:17; 3 Ne. 27:20; D&C 19:31).
- He can carry truth to the hearts of people and soften them (see 1 Ne. 2:16; 2 Ne. 33:1; Alma 24:8).
- He can enhance a person's skills and abilities to perform a task (see Ex. 31:3–5; 1 Ne. 18:1–4; D&C 46:18).
- He sometimes either constrains (impels forward) or restrains (holds back) (see 1 Ne. 7:15; 2 Ne. 28:1; 32:7; Alma 14:11; Morm. 3:16).
- He edifies (lifts or builds spiritually) both the teacher and the student (see 1 Cor. 14:12; D&C 50:22–23; 84:106).
- As one of His titles implies, He gives comfort (see John 14:26; D&C 88:3).

(*Teaching the Gospel* [Handbook for CES Teachers and Leaders] 1994, 12–13.)

CHAPTER 11
TRUE CONVERSION

In order to really teach others the gospel, we must be truly converted to it. Now is the time to gain a testimony, not three months into our missions. "Ye cannot say when ye are brought to the MTC that I will repent, that I will gain a testimony . . . Ye cannot say this, for that same spirit which doth possess you prior to the MTC will possess you after." Our true conversion must take place now. The Lord wants us *already* prepared. Like any investigator, we must first study the word—the Book of Mormon—and then make and keep covenants with the Lord. Ordinances and covenants honored bring us back into the presence of God. For true conversion to happen, we all need to feel the Spirit, become aware of it, and then make and keep commitments.

USING THE BOOK OF MORMON AS THE KEY TO CONVERSION

Although the prophets in Book of Mormon times wrote in the characters of reformed Egyptian, this is a book for our dispensation. Joseph Smith called the Book of Mormon the keystone of our religion, and then declared that "a man would get nearer to God by abiding by its precepts, than by any other book" (Introduction to the Book of Mormon).

If you know anything about building arches, you know that the keystone is the center piece of stone that holds the arch up. The purpose of the Book of Mormon is to witness that Heavenly Father is our Father and that He extends mercy and love to us, to witness of Jesus Christ, and to document how He has dealt with all of His people. This book is for you and me; it is written for everyone—those with a testimony of the gospel and those who have not learned those truths. If you learn to love it, this book will be the greatest power you have on your mission. If you learn to love and understand its teachings, you will then be able to testify of the book, and you will have great converting power.

A Divine Witness

The Book of Mormon was translated by the power of God through the Prophet Joseph Smith—who gave his life for this book. He was tarred and feathered and left for dead in Hyrum, Ohio; he was thrown in jail, and mocked and ridiculed just for bringing the book into existence. And Joseph wasn't the only prophet who suffered for the sake of the book. Abinadi was burned at the stake, and Moroni was left alone to preserve it when all his people had died. Because of the importance of the book, Enos prayed to the Lord with all of his heart that the book would come forth in this day. "Thy fathers have also required of me this thing," the Lord told Enos. "And it shall be done unto them according to their faith; for their faith was like unto thine" (Enos 1:18).

Why is the book so important? What is its purpose? The purpose of the Book of Mormon is fivefold: (1) it stands as a second testament or witness for Jesus Christ; (2) it authenticates the Bible; (3) it shows the goodness of God to His children; (4) it makes people aware of the promises that God has made to His children; and (5) it restores to earth many plain and precious truths that were lost during the Apostasy.

The first purpose, however, is primary. This book convinces people that Jesus is the Christ. "Come unto Christ, and be perfected in him" (Moro. 10:32) the scriptures invite. That is the purpose of the Book of Mormon. That is what you must know, that is what you must feel, and that is what you must understand. That knowledge and love of the book must be radiating from your very being. This is one of the reasons that you are instructed to sup from these pages for at least thirty minutes every day. You will never be the missionary you were destined to be until you love and live this book. It is the key to conversion.

Loving and Living by the Book

The Book of Mormon will never become part of your life until you delight in the word of God. "Now, we will compare the word [the Book of Mormon is the word of God] unto a seed," Alma teaches; "Now, if ye give place, that a seed may be planted in your heart" (Alma 32:28), or in other words, we take this seed, this word of God, this Book of Mormon, and put it in our hearts. (It might help to know that in Hebrew the word "heart" is *leb* or *lebab*, which interpreted means the center of the mind or the center of the soul, the decision-making center of your body; so when we yield our hearts to the Lord, what we're doing is saying, "All my decisions are the decisions Thou would make, Father. Not my will, but Thy will.")

Now back to Alma. If we give a place for the seed, which is the Book of Mormon, to be planted in our hearts (or in other words, all of our decisions will be made by the principles contained in the book), then "if it be a true seed, or a good seed, if ye do not cast it out by your unbelief, that ye will resist the Spirit of the Lord, behold, it will begin to swell within your breasts; and when you feel these swelling motions, ye will begin to say within yourselves—It must needs be that this is a good seed, or that the word is good, for it beginneth to enlarge my soul; yea, it beginneth to enlighten my understanding, yea, it beginneth to be delicious to me" (Alma 32:28).

When the Book of Mormon lives in our lives, then we will be pure disciples of Christ with great converting power, fulfilling the destiny that President Ezra Taft Benson described so eloquently when he said, "I have a vision of homes alerted, classes alive, pulpits aflame with the Spirit of the Book of Mormon messages. . . . I have a vision of the whole Church getting nearer to God by abiding the precepts of the Book of Mormon" ("Flooding the Earth with the Book of Mormon," *Ensign*, Nov. 1988, 4–6).

In the same article, President Benson also said, "This sacred volume of scripture needs to become more central in our preaching, our teaching, and our missionary work" (*Ensign*, Nov. 1988, 4–6). He counseled us to flood the earth with the Book of Mormon, adding this call to action: "I challenge our mission leaders to show their missionaries how to challenge their contacts to read the Book of Mormon and pray about it. . . . I challenge the homes of Israel to display on some of their walls, great quotations and scenes from the Book of Mormon" (*Ensign*, Nov. 1988, 4–6).

In early Church history, some missionaries returned from their missions and were reproved. "You have treated lightly the things you have received," they were told. "Which vanity and unbelief have brought the whole church under condemnation" (D&C 84:54–55). We must lift this condemnation individually and collectively.

Elder Bruce R. McConkie said, "The Book of Mormon contains that portion of the Lord's word which is needed to prove the divinity of his great latter-day work, and which is needed to teach the basic doctrines of salvation to mankind" ("This Generation Shall Have My Word Through You," *Ensign*, June 1980, 54). In using this powerful book with our investigators, we have the promise of President Ezra Taft Benson: "The Lord will manifest the truthfulness of it, by the power of the Holy Ghost" ("Cleansing the Inner Vessel," *Ensign*, May 1986, 4–6).

A Powerful Tool of Conversion

It's important that you and I develop an abiding faith in the Lord's promise that if people will ask with a sincere heart, having faith in Christ, the truthfulness of the Book of Mormon will be given to them (see Moro. 10:3–5). Think about what it means if we can accept the Book of Mormon in our lives: if the Book of Mormon is true, then Joseph Smith was a prophet; if Joseph Smith was a prophet, the First Vision really did take place; if the First Vision was a reality, the priesthood was restored; if the priesthood was restored, the Doctrine and Covenants, Pearl of Great Price, and other scriptures are true; not only that, but the Church, which was established by Joseph Smith, is true; and so we're led by true prophets of the Lord today. We will know all that when we accept the Book of Mormon!

We must put the Book of Mormon first. When we root ourselves in the love of the people, or the love of the Church, or the love of the sociality and friendships we feel at Church, what happens the first time we feel a lack of love? We fall away. But when we are rooted in Christ and His love, we are rooted in something solid and secure, because Christ's love never changes; it's always there. The love of our Heavenly Father is the same. The Book of Mormon plays a crucial role in rooting people to Christ. Every aspect of a person's testimony is anchored in place by the Book of Mormon. Think of that: every aspect of a person's testimony is held in place by what is found in the pages of the Book of Mormon.

If we teach the Book of Mormon, we teach nothing but the gospel of Jesus Christ. If we teach the gospel of Christ with power, we will be rooted to Christ. If we are rooted to Christ, we are rooted to the Atonement. If we are rooted to the Atonement, we are rooted to the gospel. If we're rooted to the gospel, we're rooted to faith, repentance, baptism, covenant making, and the gift of the Holy Ghost.

Feasting on the Word of God

Remember that before anyone we teach can sense the power and divinity of the Book of Mormon for themselves, they must sense it in us. We must delight in the word of God. We must love the Book of Mormon. We must feast upon its words. We must be truly converted.

When the Book of Mormon becomes delicious to you, you will sparkle. You will be excited. You'll visit your investigators and say, "Oh, I just had to drop by and read you this part here; this is so good I can hardly wait to tell you!" If you don't feel that way, your investigators won't feel that way. Now perhaps you can begin to understand why one precious half hour every day is spent supping from the pages of this book of books. Learn to love the book, and you'll not only love to live its teachings yourself, but you'll love to teach it.

President Benson said, "I would particularly urge you to read again and again, the Book of Mormon and ponder and apply its teachings" ("To the 'Youth of the Noble Birthright,'" *Ensign*, May 1986, 43). Isn't that interesting? Ponder and apply its teachings. I try to do that every day, pondering the scriptures every night and then applying a scripture in my life every day, and even recording it in my journal. This daily application of scriptures can absolutely change our lives.

Nephi understood this principle: "For my soul delighteth in the scriptures, and my heart pondereth them" (2 Ne. 4:15). President Benson also understood: "Reread the Book of Mormon so that we might more fully come unto Christ, be committed to him, centered in him, and consumed in him" (*The Teachings of Ezra Taft Benson*, 11).

Do you see now what will happen with studying the Book of Mormon? When Christ comes into our lives, we are born of God, and we'll also be strengthened through the Book of Mormon. If we are conscientious in our study of the Book of Mormon, we will not be susceptible to Satan's enticings. I promise you that if you'll earnestly and prayerfully ponder, and steadfastly read the Book of Mormon and live it, the adversary will have no effect upon you. And unless you do that, you will not be strong.

Why is this? How do we become spiritually strong? How do we grow in faith? The answer is always the same: the word of God applied in our lives makes us strong. It makes our spirits strong. In other words, when we delight, they'll be delighted.

We need to realize that when we're reading is when the Lord will testify to us it's true. We don't read all 531 pages and then say, "Okay, I've finished reading. Now I pray." It's an ongoing daily process to know that the Book of Mormon is true. We don't need to wait until we've finished reading to start asking!

If we are sincere after we've carefully followed these steps, things will begin to happen. We will ponder and pray about the contents of the Book of Mormon, and its teachings will become important in our lives. When Parley P. Pratt received the Book of Mormon he said that he couldn't eat or sleep; all he wanted to do was read the book. Parley P. Pratt was sincere, and so was qualified to receive an answer from the Lord. If we are sincere, we'll ponder the contents of the Book of Mormon, and by means of the Spirit we will agree with the teachings. We will become truly converted, rooted in the word of God.

One of the greatest truths we'll ever teach people is that they are children of God the Father, and that He has a plan that provides us eternal life and happiness. This is fundamental to the gospel of Jesus Christ and is taught in the first discussion. So many people in the world don't even realize this. And when we teach this and pray about it, the Lord will tell us it's true; we'll receive answers and know that the doctrine is right.

RENEW AND REMEMBER OUR OWN COMMITMENTS

As missionaries, and as future parents in Zion, we must remember that we don't change any faster than we make and keep commitments. The Lord calls them covenants. Our exaltation is determined by how well we have kept our baptismal, our priesthood, and our temple covenants.

And when we keep those covenants, the promises and blessings are ours. I have learned that when covenants are deepened because our commitment is strong, our lives are different. If in your lives—either at this moment as elders and sisters, or later—you find yourselves vacillating, look deep into your souls and check your level of commitment to your covenants. And when your level of commitment to your covenants has deepened to where you feel that it is life eternal to keep them, you will be a missionary for life. You will help many souls come unto Christ. When you make covenants with the Lord at that altar in the temple, and you become a mother or father, and find yourselves missionaries of a whole different sort, you'll never be totally converted until you learn to make and keep covenants by committing yourselves to the Lord.

Our blessings here and hereafter are dependent upon keeping the covenants we make with God. We recovenant each week as we partake of the sacrament. This is how Heavenly Father helps us—by continually reminding us of our commitments to His law and His covenants. The Spirit will help us keep those covenants, and keeping those covenants will bring us back into His presence.

We are a covenant-making church. We are a covenant-making people. The gospel of Jesus Christ, the plan of happiness was based and framed upon a series of covenants and promises. In the premortal world we covenanted and agreed to the plan of our Heavenly Father as presented by the Savior, Jesus Christ, Jehovah. We were then given the opportunity to come to this earth to prove ourselves. The very essence of the plan is the gospel of Jesus Christ—based and framed upon the love of God for His children, and as the love of Christ for his brothers and sisters. This love of God is the very basis of our happiness here upon the earth. In 1 Nephi 8:10 it states, "Whose fruit it was desirable to make one happy." "Happiness," as Joseph Smith said, "is the object and design of our existence" (HC 5:134–35).

What is this state? Can we say every day that we are happy? Sometimes we use the word "happy" as a sense of well-being. Happiness is a state of existence due to the possession of the love of God and the love of Christ. We can possess this love as we hold to the iron rod. The iron rod is the word of God. The words of Christ will lead us to this fruit which is in fact the love of God. The Atonement was Christ's and God the Father's expression of Their love. How do we accept the Atonement of Christ? We accept the Atonement of Christ through covenants. Everything in the Church is based upon the covenants. The Church is the kingdom of God on earth, and within it lies the foundation, the gospel of Jesus Christ, which flows into our very beings as we accept and embrace and keep our covenants. The covenant of baptism is the gate to the straight and narrow path and is the beginning covenant of mortality that leads us back to our Heavenly Father—for strait is the gate and narrow is the way that leads us back (see Matt. 7:14). When Nicodemus asked what it took, Jesus reminded him, "Except a man be born of water and of the Spirit he cannot enter . . ." (John 3:5). The gateway is baptism. This is why it is so important to be converted ourselves, so we can help lead others to this gate.

Let us this day remember our covenants, remember our purposes, keep the vision of who we are—the children of God. As we accept the covenants and enter into them, we become like the people of King Benjamin, willing to embrace the fullness of the gospel of Jesus Christ.

CONCLUSION

According to James R. Harris, an author and teacher at Brigham Young University:

> There are six universal elements of conversion experience. These elements seem to have both a logical and a chronological relationship to each other.
>
> *First,* one must become aware of the reality and power of God.
>
> *Second,* an awareness of God as an active, imminent cause in the affairs of men, possessing all wisdom and almighty power, imbues man with a consciousness of human weakness.
>
> *Third,* further introspection will cause a man to conclude that he has been alienated from God because of his personal transgressions of divine law. His guilt is a product of his new consciousness of God and is therefore called a "godly sorrow for sin." Man is brokenhearted.

Fourth, man exhibits a contrite spirit which is often expressed in the question, "Lord, what shall I do?" He will do anything that is required to obtain the desired reconciliation with his Savior.

Fifth, when the requirements, given in answer to the above questions, have been met, man may know the joy of his redemption, enjoy peace of conscience through the companionship of the Spirit which is his witness of divine love and approval.

Sixth, he will desire to give others an opportunity to partake of this exceedingly great joy. He will be a zealous and fruitful witness of his personal Savior.

I know that these principles are true, that God works with men today as he worked with them in all past dispensations. There are eternal elements of the conversion experience. I have tasted the bitterness of hell and I have rejoiced in the joy of my redemption. I bear you my testimony that Jesus the Christ atoned for my sins and for yours, but to benefit fully from his atonement we must come unto him and experience in the process these six elements of conversion. May the Lord bless us all to continue to grow in spirit through conversion experiences.

(James R. Harris, "Patterns of Conversion in the Book of Mormon" [Provo: Brigham Young University Press, 1968], 61.)

Conversion happens when our hearts are softened and touched by the Spirit. The word is planted, and when nourished it begins to grow and people change. We must make the mighty change—we must be new creatures. We must be born again. As missionaries, it is our joy and glory to help in this process that other people might come unto Christ and be perfected in Him.

CHAPTER 12
MISSIONARIES FOR LIFE—TRUE DISCIPLES OF CHRIST

Elders and sisters return from their missions with much joy and satisfaction. Words from the pulpit sound like, "It was the best two years," or "It was the greatest two years," or "It was the happiest time of my life." Why do missionaries say those words?

WHY THE BEST TWO YEARS?

It's because they are devoted to the Lord; they have spent all their time and all their effort in His behalf, blessing people. They are happy because they spent their lives in building up the kingdom of God. And this means they are helping people come unto Christ. On missions, we all work hard. We're busy. We have a regular schedule. We're always thinking of others and praying for others and pleading with the Lord that they'll come unto Christ.

Sometimes there are days that are frustrating because people are not hospitable. Sometimes we feel persecuted. Sometimes people don't make the commitments. Often times we don't have enough money and are off our budget. But we don't pursue worldly things. We don't seek after cars, or clothes, or notoriety or fame, or worry about who's winning the game, but just "Who can I bless today?" Every morning we wake up, we search the scriptures for an hour alone and then for another hour with our companion. Then we pray morning, noon, and night. We pray for our investigators, we pray for our companions, we pray for the whole world that they might be happy. We pray to do the Father's will and build up His kingdom. Our lives are focused. We set goals and we make plans: "How many people can we find today? How many are we going to invite to church? How many copies of the Book of Mormon can we place?" This results in preparing people to come unto Christ, and makes our lives focused on one thing, and that is the Lord Jesus Christ and His kingdom.

As we attempt to do this, we are nurtured by the Spirit. We are led by the Spirit. We teach and testify by the Spirit. We enjoy all the blessings of the Spirit from choosing to do good, to do justly, to walk humbly, to judge righteously, to enlighten our minds, to fill our souls with joy, to give us love, peace, long-suffering, gentleness, goodness, faith, meekness, and temperance. As missionaries we can enjoy these feelings of the Spirit's companionship. That's why we feel so good building up His kingdom—serving our fellowmen and the Lord every moment of our lives.

Why do we do this? Because of the Atonement of Jesus Christ. Christ died so that we might live. For the whole world, for all mankind, He suffered and died that we might return to the presence of our Heavenly Father. And that is why we serve. So, we are saviors on Mount Zion. The Lord said we are the "light unto the world, and to be the saviors of men" (D&C 103:9). We recognize the worth of souls. How great shall be our joy over a soul that repenteth? (see D&C 18:10–16). And how much greater will it be if many souls repent? And in particular, the Lord says how happy He is, and how much joy He has over a soul that repents (see D&C 18:10, 13–16). If we achieve our goals, we have the joy and the fruit of our labors.

I'll never forget the time when two elders were struggling. It was 10:30 at night and the phone rang. Now the missionaries are supposed to be asleep at 10:30, but on the other end of the phone I heard this weeping voice. And I said, "Elder, are you okay?"

He said, "Yes, I think so."

I said, "Is your companion okay?"

"Yes, he's okay."

So then I asked, "What's the matter?"

"Sally (we'll call her Sally) is not going to be baptized; I just can't stand it."

I said, "Oh Elder, I'm sorry, but she'll be okay."

And then all of a sudden the Spirit came to me and said, "She'll be okay, she'll be baptized."

I said, "Give me her phone number." And so the next morning at 8:30 I called her up and I said, "Sally, how do you feel about being baptized?"

She said, "Oh, I'm so nervous, President Pinegar, I just don't know."

I said, "Well, how do you feel about the Book of Mormon when you read it?"

"Oh, I love the Book of Mormon, it's just so good. I want to be good when I read it."

"Well, how do you feel about the Prophet Joseph Smith?"

"Oh, he's a prophet."

I said, "That is so good. Have you had a chance to attend church?"

"Oh yes, I've been to church; it's so nice."

I said, "You know what? Since you know this, and you feel this, that's the Spirit telling you that it's true. It's important to follow Christ and keep His commandments and take His name upon you. You know, I was looking forward to coming to your baptism on Sunday night."

"You were?"

I said, "Yes."

Then she said, "Well, okay, I'll be baptized, but I told the elders last night I wouldn't be baptized."

I said, "Don't worry, I'll call them and let them know and they'll call you right back." So I called the elders. I said, "Hello, Elders, it's President Pinegar. Everything's okay, Sally will be baptized."

"Sally will be baptized?" they asked.

I said, "Yes."

Then I promised I'd be there. Well, as I drove up to the Croyden chapel, and one elder was on the outside stairs waiting for us. It was as if they were the brand-new parents of a perfect child. We walked in and the elders said, "President and Sister Pinegar, this is Sally." You would think she was the queen of the world. The worth of souls is great. So, when you're a missionary, your mind is thinking only of blessing other people. When you achieve your goals and you have the fruit of your labors, bringing souls unto Christ, you are consumed with the Spirit. You have an overwhelming desire to do good.

On your mission you continually receive support and praise for all that you are doing: letters from parents and friends, the support of the bishopric; your mission president always praising and thanking you for building up the kingdom; confirmation from the Spirit of the great things that you're doing; letters of praise and support and gratitude from converts; and above all, you feel the love of God, knowing that you're on the errand of the Lord Jesus Christ. And these wholesome relationships and feelings you have aren't built upon lust, or greed, or power, or vanity, they're built on your desire to help someone. Yes, as a missionary you have the vision of the work of the Lord, to bring to pass the immortality and eternal life of men. You are always applying correct principles to your life. That's what happens on a mission.

MAINTAINING THE VISION—WHY NOT MORE THAN TWO YEARS?

But when you're not on your mission, things are different—things are really different. You're not quite as organized before you go or when you get back. You feel like you're home—your mission is only two years and you don't have to stay focused on the Lord and His work more than that. And that is a BIG mistake. Missions are for *life*. And, guess what else? There's not near as much praise and appreciation. We become kind of self-serving, like, "I've got to do this, and I've got to do that, and I've got to do this, and I need to go over there . . ." and it's all about me, me, me, rather than looking out for others. Some of us are still in this phase, and some of us are returning to it after our missions. But the point of "raising the bar" is to avoid this in the first place. We are to become better, more dedicated servants to the Lord, regardless of whether our mission is five years away, or if we've been home for five years. Missionaries always say it was the best two years of their lives. But why should we only have *two* best years? Why not live our best lives in the service of God continually?

When I was a bishop a few years ago, an elder had just returned from his mission about five or six months before, and he came in and said, "Bishop Ed, I've got to talk to you right now." He was a very big, strong football player. He said, "I'm not happy anymore," and he began to cry. "My mission was great, and now I don't know what's going wrong. Life is not good. It's the pits. I just wish I was back there, and yet I want to be here. I'm just, I'm just . . ." He was frustrated, overwhelmed, and downright discouraged. And then he blurted out, "And I know why. I'm not doing what the Lord wants me to do. Bishop Ed, every day on my mission I searched the scriptures, I studied with my companion, I prayed with real intent to bless people's lives. Now I don't do anything like that at all."

Too many missionaries come home saying, "I've got to adjust to a new way of living because I'm going to live differently now," and that is a mistake. *Life* is our mission before and after we are formally called. We came on this earth to perform a mission, to live here, to help people be happy, and sometimes, when we're out of the mode of full-time proselyting missionary, we forget that we're always a missionary. The young women of the Church stand up and say, "We are daughters of our Heavenly Father, who loves us, and we love Him. We will stand as witnesses of God at all times and in all things, and in all places as we strive to live the Young Women values . . ." (*Young Women Theme*). You think about that. Young women between twelve and eighteen have the values and standards to stand as witnesses for God at all times, in all things, and all places. Now, that teaches us a principle. We must make our life as a missionary part and parcel of our whole life. In other words, the only way to be happy is to always live by the Spirit. Your life must be a Spirit-directed life. It's a different time in life but the same principles are involved.

In the mission field, you wanted to find people to whom you could teach the gospel. The rest of life is the same way. As we follow the Spirit, we'll all of a sudden realize, "I am a son or daughter of God, the Eternal Father. I am a disciple of Jesus Christ. My duty and obligation here on the earth is always the same: to help people." Whether as a home teacher, or a visiting teacher, Sunday School teacher, Primary teacher—our job is to help people. Well, the same principles you learn in the mission field apply in the family, at work, at play, and at school. You find out how people are feeling. You present messages. You help them recognize the Spirit because you have taken the time to build a relationship of trust, so your credibility is strong. You follow up and see how they're feeling. You help them come to Christ.

Keep the Commandments

So how do we maintain our focus on Christ and building up the kingdom? The Lord, through the Apostle John in the New Testament, said, "If ye love me, keep my commandments" (John 14:15). This becomes an important solution to being happy before, during, and after your mission.

As our emphasis becomes that of a lifelong mission, one thing should be constant—that we do Heavenly Father's will. If we don't, and it's not in our plans, then righteousness is not ours and we lose. And what do we lose? We lose happiness. King Benjamin said if we are righteous we'll be happy. And if we continue to press forward in righteousness, we'll enter into a state of never-ending happiness (see Mosiah 2:41).

Goals and Self-Discipline

The phases of life outside your full-time mission should merely be an extension of your growth, not a separate, compartmentalized time of life. Never compartmentalize the gospel of Jesus Christ. How do we avoid doing this? The solution is clear. We have the Spirit, but we must organize every needful thing. We must have the vision of what we want to accomplish. In the mission field you plan every day: who to visit, who to see, who to bless, and how to help. At home you also need to plan out your day: go to work, visit your home teaching family or the women you visit teach, read your scriptures, pray for your family, etc. You make a list, a little list of planning to organize every needful time and every needful thing. Your use of time will be better, your educational experience will be better, and your life will be better.

I'll never forget one elder. He'd returned home from his mission and he was going to school, and he wrote me a letter.

> Dear President Pinegar,
>
> School's going great, everything's good, life is good, life after the mission is terrific. You know what, President? You know when you taught us to set goals and make plans? I thought, well that works in the mission field; it ought to work in school. So, I took our planner and where it had everything to do with teaching

people, I would substitute classes and work and educational experiences and things, and I made my plan to achieve in all those areas. President, I just thought you'd want to know that I got a 4.0 this semester, and boy, do I feel good.

In other words, he was happy because he had achieved, because he had set his goals and made his plans.

Goals are important, and so is the self-discipline we need to accomplish them. Most importantly, we must remember that as we make our goals and our plans, we must balance our lives. Intellectual, social, emotional, physical, and above all, spiritual areas are all important. We can balance them so everything has adequate time in relationship to our life.

Prayer and Fasting

There are three major things we must do in order to know every needful thing and stay strong in the kingdom. Too many of us are casual in our gospel study, casual in our prayers, casual in our attendance at church, casual in our building up the kingdom of God, casual in living a Christlike life, and casual in avoiding and overcoming temptation. Mighty prayer and fasting is absolutely essential to your adjusting as a missionary. The biggest problem is temptation. The Lord said to pray because Satan wants to sift us as wheat (see 3 Ne. 18:15, 18). If we're not praying to avoid temptation, we're in trouble. As we learn in Helaman 3:35, we need to pray to increase our humility and faith. We must pray, even as the Nephites prayed, for the desire to have the gift of the Holy Ghost (see 3 Ne. 19:9). For the gift of the Holy Ghost will tell you not some, not most, but *all* things what you should do. Wouldn't you like to be able to just know at any given moment, all the things that are important in your life to do? (see 2 Ne. 32:5)

A scripture in Alma explains how easy it is to be eligible for the direction of the Spirit. As we learn in Alma 37:37, we should "counsel with the Lord in all thy doings." So, when we are on or off our mission, we counsel with the Lord in all our doings, and He will direct us for good. "Yea, when thou liest down at night lie down unto the Lord, that he may watch over you in your sleep; and when thou risest in the morning let thy heart be full of thanks unto God; and if

ye do these things, ye shall be lifted up at the last day" (Alma 37:37).
If we counsel with the Lord morning, noon, and night, we'll be in
tune with the Spirit enough to be directed just as we are on our
missions.

Remember when Nephi went back to get the plates? He said,
"And I was led by the Spirit, not knowing beforehand the things
which I should do" (1 Ne. 4:6). The Spirit comes to us as we have
faith, love, and obedience, and pray with all our heart, might, mind,
and soul for this gift. Now the fruit of fasting and prayer—from
Moroni 7:48, which says pray with all the energy of your heart that
you might be filled with this—is charity. Remember the love of God?
The fruit of the tree which is desirable above all other things to make
one happy? Well, those who partake of this fruit are happy because
they've come unto Christ and partaken of the love of God. That's the
difference, you see. When we come to the tree of life and partake of
that love, we're happy. We're happy on our mission. Well, we should
be doing the same thing at home before and after our mission in
order to achieve that same kind of happiness. We will start to become
like Christ. We will receive direction in our life. Our faith and
humility will become firm and strong. We will overcome and avoid
temptation. We will help others come unto Christ. We will help those
who are straying. We will become righteous. We will become happy,
and life is sweet if we pray with real intent, having faith in God. If
our prayers are casual, so likewise will our life be casual—not focused
on the kingdom of God.

Search the Scriptures

The next thing that will ensure we always maintain the vision is
to search the scriptures. Remember that elder? "I wasn't saying my
prayers and I wasn't searching the scriptures." The scriptures will tell
us all things that we should do (see 2 Ne. 32:3). We're cautioned, or
implored, to live by every word that proceedeth forth from the mouth
of God. When we hold to the iron rod, the mists of darkness, or
temptation, will not get us, but we'll be able to press forward and
partake of the tree of life. Yes, the word of God has power. It has a
greater power to cause men to do that which is just, more than
anything else (see Alma 31:5). That's how powerful the word is. How

can we throw away such power and revert back to a lifestyle of not searching the scriptures and not expect to feel bad?

The only way we can stay on the strait and narrow path is by making and keeping commitments. We must always remember what is taught in Helaman 12:2–3, that due to the ease of the way and the comfort which the people enjoyed, guess what happened? They forgot God. When we aren't on our mission, things may become too easy and comfortable, we may find that we will forget; hence, the blessings of happiness are not ours. Always remember, as we go to sacrament meeting and partake of the sacrament, we covenant to take His name upon us, remember to keep His commandments. As we remember, then we will be happy because our lives will be focused on our Savior Jesus Christ, no matter what phase we are in, and we shall have His Spirit to be with us.

Always Serve

You can't coast on or off your mission and live on your life of past service. To feel the Spirit of the Lord and feel good, you must continue in service. How then do you live the gospel all the time, especially when you're not serving a full-time mission as a set-apart missionary?

One way is through the temple. Sometimes, as we become complacent, we fail to go back and refresh our minds with the temple and temple worship. As you go to the temple, in the Lord's house, you will find peace and you will find happiness, because this too is an important form of service. Going to the temple will also help reinforce your commitment to your covenants, and you will remember 2 Nephi 31:19–21 and endure to the end.

As you find yourself enduring cheerfully, remember those still trying to endure to the end of their missions, or recent converts who may need some buoying up. Write some missionaries. Write some new converts to help them and strengthen them in all that they do. Service, either to those in the field, or here at home for those you meet, will help you keep your focus on the Lord instead of yourself.

Not long ago I wasn't feeling so good. I was getting near retirement and I was worried about whether I had enough money to retire. When you get old, you start worrying about things like that because there's not going to be a job, and social security is small, and the little retirement I had set aside was making me kind of nervous. I was thinking about it all the time. I was obsessed with having enough money to live on. I became unhappy because I'd lost my focus. Besides that, the stock market had gone down horribly to the point where I had lost a fair amount of money. Well, I prayed and focused on what to do. With prayer the answer came. "Ed, teach your missionary preparation class with every fiber of your being, bless people's lives." Within almost minutes, because my attitude had changed, I began to feel good again and I was happy. I smiled and I was full of more joy because I wasn't thinking about me and my problem, but rather, "Who can I bless? How can I help?"

As we do all things with the Lord, it's important to remember to be friendly, to look to those we can bless in our families. If we're in the mode of service to our family, we'll be surprised at how happy and healthy we will be. And remember this: every day is a test. Every day is a test to prove ourselves worthy to return to the presence of the Lord. Every day, prepare to meet God.

You're Always a Missionary

Every moment is a missionary moment. We do not compartmentalize living a Christlike life into "missions," and "pre- or post-mission." We set goals in many areas of our lives that are compatible to bless mankind and build up the kingdom of God, and in doing so we get closer to our Heavenly Father.

Continually building up the kingdom of God requires desire, positive attitude, and work ethic—just like on our missions. It must become our walk and talk. We may all do it differently according to our situations and personalities; but we must eventually open our mouths in order that people might be led to the Lord Jesus Christ.

We can't assume that the extra opportunity and privilege of missionary work belongs only to those who serve full-time missions, that we've done our part and now it's up to everybody else. There's a little story about that called "Teamwork," and it goes as follows:

> There are four people named Everybody, Somebody, Anybody, and Nobody. There was an important job to be done and Everybody was asked to do it. Everybody was sure Somebody

would do it. Anybody could have done it, but Nobody did it. Somebody got angry about that, because it was Everybody's job. Everybody thought Anybody could have done it, but Nobody realized that Everybody wouldn't do it. It ended up that Everybody blamed Somebody when Nobody did what Anybody could have done.

—Anonymous

This bit of humor points out a problem we have in the Church today. Everybody prays that their nice neighbors across the street will join the Church, but they're also hoping that somebody else will be the first to cross that endless chasm and strike up a gospel conversation. We must not be afraid to open our mouths.

There are numbers of ways we can preach the gospel in our now-busy lives, even with all of our other responsibilities. Start with your own family and work out from there. Write your testimony in the front cover of the Book of Mormon and give it to someone—even friends or relatives (gasp!), or have it translated into several languages and send it out to missionaries in the field. Place the Book of Mormon in your local library. Fellowship people at work, strike up conversations on your way somewhere, or in lines at the grocery store. Fellowship new converts—attend their baptisms and welcome them with open arms. Remember, life goes on after a "no." It's not the end of the world. Just keep loving them, serving them, and keep building up the kingdom.

CONCLUSION

We are all always serving the mission of life. Building up the kingdom of God is still a priority, with family and friends, and at school and work. Now we simply broaden our focus a little. Our lives are always dedicated to the threefold mission of the Church—to perfect the Saints, redeem the dead, and proclaim the gospel.

We should treat everyone like an investigator. Why do we treat investigators so nicely? Because we want them to come into the kingdom. Well you know what? If we treat everybody that way, life would be more sweet in all that we do, and we would all help each other come into the kingdom.

Remember to stay focused on living the gospel every day. Rely on the Lord. Be patient in all things and be sure that your expectation of others is not so high that you cannot make life fun and happy. Above all, stay busy. Never, ever lower your standards. Guilt and sin will bring great sorrow.

You might say to yourself, "Well, I know those things." That's right, you do know everything you have read, but the difference is, will you remember and apply these things and apply them to your life? Life will be sweet if you continue on your course of coming unto Christ, accepting and respecting His atoning sacrifice, and being perfected by Him in all that you do.

CHAPTER 13
JOY OF THE WORK

In August of 1975, President Benson gave a marvelous talk at the Tokyo, Japan Area Conference. In that talk he quoted President Spencer W. Kimball on the need to enhance our vision of missionary work: "We must raise our sights, and get a vision of the magnitude and urgency of this great missionary work" ("Safety in the Face of Wickedness," Tokyo Japan area conference, 8–10 Aug. 1975). Now we are not only raising our sights, but the standard of missionary work too. The Church in this dispensation is to proclaim the gospel, to perfect the Saints, and redeem the dead. Why is this so important? Everything that the Church, which is the kingdom of God, does here upon the earth is for one purpose, and that is to assist in Heavenly Father's work. "For behold, this is my work and my glory—to bring to pass the immortality and eternal life of man" (Moses 1:39). That means everyone. Everything Heavenly Father does, and will do, is so that you and I can be happy and return to His presence forever.

The worth of souls is great in the sight of God. He needs good, strong servants who will care for these valuable souls. How great shall be your joy with those people whom you help come unto Christ. And if your joy be great with one, think how great it will be with many (see D&C 18:10–16). In other words, Heavenly Father's priority is His children. Now, I don't know what that does for you, but that gives me eternal self-esteem because I, Ed Jolley Pinegar, am Heavenly Father's son, and you are His sons and daughters. And the greatest thing you'll ever do on this earth is to help His children return home. "But seek ye first the kingdom of God, and his righteousness; and all these things shall be added unto you" (Matt. 6:33). In the Joseph

Smith translation of the Bible that verse now reads, "Seek ye first to build up the kingdom of God, and to establish his righteousness; and all these things shall be added unto you" (JS—M 6:33). Build up the kingdom! What is the kingdom made of? Men and women. You and me. When you bless someone's life, you elevate your own life. When you've "done it unto one of the least of these my brethren," the Savior said, you've "done it unto me" (see Matt. 25:40). We must catch the vision of the worth of souls. Once you understand the worth of a soul, you'll want to share the gospel of Jesus Christ. You'll want to help other people be happy because it's the only way you'll ever be happy on this earth and in the hereafter. If you don't seek to serve, and seek to bless, it's very difficult to grow.

The sons of Mosiah and Alma were not only inactive in the Church, but were engaged in active persecution. Alma the Younger was the ringleader. However, they all repented of their sins, became totally converted, and became great and wonderful missionaries. I love Alma, Ammon, Omner, Himni, and Aaron. Did they have the vision of missionary work? Did they care about other people's souls? "Now [the sons of Mosiah] were desirous that salvation should be declared to every creature, for they could not bear that any human soul should perish; yea, even the very thoughts that any soul should endure endless torment did cause them to quake and tremble" (Mosiah 28:3). Do you feel that way? Do you quake and tremble if you see someone doing something wrong? Would you hurry and say a prayer if somebody were struggling and not coming to church, and say, "Heavenly Father, bless Billy, or Bobby, or Sally, or Suzy, and please help them catch the vision and please bless their lives," instead of saying, "They deserve what they get." You'll always know how Christlike you are by how much concern you have for others. For that is the barometer of your love and Christlike capacity.

The sons of Mosiah had great concern for their fellowmen. They knew the worth of souls. They had the vision in their mind. Alma the Younger felt likewise: "I know that which the Lord hath commanded me, and I glory in it. I do not glory of myself, but I glory in that which the Lord hath commanded me; yea, and this is my glory, that perhaps I may be an instrument in the hands of God to bring some soul to repentance; and this is my joy" (Alma 29:9). Now he didn't say, "When I graduate from college with a 4.0, then I'll feel good. When I'm the captain of the football team or do a slam dunk, then I'll be okay." He said, "If I can just be an instrument in the hands of the Lord, this is my glory and my joy."

He goes on to say in verse 10, "And behold, when I see many of my brethren truly penitent [or repentant] and coming to the Lord their God, then is my soul filled with joy; then do I remember what the Lord has done for me, yea, even that he hath heard my prayer; yea, then do I remember his merciful arm which he extended towards me."

The joy of helping people repent—that's the vision. Why do you think all the missionaries come home and say the same thing at the pulpit? "It was the happiest eighteen months of my life. It was the greatest two years of my life." I mean, do you like getting up at 6:30 A.M. and working twelve hours a day, every day for eighteen to twenty-four months, not watching any movies or TV? Hooray, hooray, hooray! Great missionaries have the vision—that's why they work so hard.

One time I was talking with an elderly gentlemen who was about seventy or eighty years old. He related this conversation with Elder Haight. He said, "Well, Elder Haight, I'm so old I might die on my mission." Elder Haight said, "What a great place to die." Think about it. There could be no better thing to do or place to be than serving your God and your fellowmen.

Now, are you catching the vision? The vision of the work and the vision of yourself regarding the work? The Whitmer brothers, John and Peter, came to see the Prophet Joseph, wondering what would be the most important thing they could do. Joseph received Doctrine and Covenants 15–16 in response. They are almost identical: "And now, behold, I say unto you [Elders and Sisters], that the thing which will be of the most worth unto you will be to declare repentance unto this people, that you may bring souls unto me, that you may rest with them in the kingdom of my Father. Amen" (D&C 16:6). That is the greatest thing we can ever do.

We have eight children in our family. Sister Pinegar and I were blessed with a large family, and I want you to know all of them came on this earth as investigators. We taught all eight of them, and all eight were baptized. Therefore, we have eight converts in our family.

Everywhere you go, you are teaching the gospel by principle, by precept, and by example. That's the vision. This earth was made only to accommodate the vision of saving souls; and that's why you, the noble and great, were preserved to come forth at this time, to do all these wonderful things.

On October 3, 1918, the Prophet Joseph F. Smith received section 138 of the Doctrine and Covenants. "I observed that they were also among the noble and great ones who were chosen in the beginning to be rulers in the Church of God. Even before they [or you] were born, they, with many others, received their first lessons in the world of spirits and were prepared to come forth in the due time of the Lord to labor in his vineyard for the salvation of the souls of men" (D&C 138:55–56). It is so important that you stay worthy and prepare to do so!

I hope you understand the vision of the work, and that you are starting to understand the vision of your responsibility in building up the kingdom of God. It is greater than it has ever been, so we must be greater than we have ever been. When you were baptized you covenanted to be willing "to stand as witnesses of God at all times and in all things and in all places" (Mosiah 18:9). To stand as a witness for God always. What do witnesses do? We testify. What do we testify of? That God is our Father, Jesus is the Christ, the Book of Mormon is true, Joseph Smith is a prophet, the gospel has been restored, the true Church is on the earth today, and we are led by a living prophet. We are witnesses. We testify. That's our duty and our joy.

"For they [you and me] were set to be a light unto the world" (D&C 103:9). The light of the world is the Lord Jesus Christ. The light that we possess is the amount of light the Lord Jesus Christ gave us. So, you are sent to be a light unto the world. But that's only part of it. The rest of the verse reads, "And to be the saviors of men; And inasmuch as they are not the saviors of men," in other words, if you're not out there with your light, helping people come unto Christ, "they [you and I] are as salt that has lost its savor" (v. 10), or become impure or have no value.

If you, as the salt of the earth, don't hold up this light, you've lost your savor. "And [are] thenceforth good for nothing but to be cast out and trodden under foot of men" (v. 10). Life is serious business. Our business on this earth is to help Heavenly Father build His kingdom by blessing our brothers and sisters, and that's it. That's what we're here for.

When I was president of the MTC, I remember watching all the missionaries coming in, and I'd just almost want to cry because I'd see them as the Lord's anointed. They would prepare, and they would go out and serve with all their heart, might, mind, and soul: "And ye shall go forth in the power of my Spirit, preaching my gospel, two by two, in my name, lifting up your voices as with the sound of a trump, declaring my word like unto angels of God" (D&C 42:6). That is wonderful. You go out like angels of God. Do you know what some ministering angels do? Many ministering angels call people to repentance. Missionaries are to preach the gospel of Jesus Christ and help people to have faith unto repentance that they might be saved. That's what missionaries do.

THE LORD WILL HELP YOU

"Treasure up in your minds continually the words of life, and it shall be given you in the very hour that portion that shall be meted unto every man" (D&C 84:85). "For it shall be given you in the very hour, yea, in the very moment, what ye shall say" (D&C 100:6). The Lord is with you when you are a missionary (see D&C 84:86–87). The key for all this to happen, as missionaries, is to have the Spirit. For without the Spirit, you cannot preach, you cannot teach, you cannot understand, and you cannot be lead. The Spirit is the key. And with the Spirit you can do all things because the Spirit will direct you. It is the Spirit that will convert.

Let me illustrate these points with an experience I had some years ago. It was about 1969 when a young girl named Susan Gerszewski came to see me. "Bishop, you've got to take my name off the records of the Church."

I said, "Oh, Susan, what's wrong?"

"My brothers think I'm a dork for being here at BYU, and I can't stand the pressure when I go home and my parents are wondering what's gone wrong with me."

And then all of a sudden, the Lord stepped in and words came out of my mouth like this: "Susan, I promise you that if you stay faithful, your brothers will join the Church and your parents' hearts will soften." Now how could I say that? I couldn't. Only the Lord could.

She said, "Oh, I just don't know, Bishop, I just don't know."

I said, "Well, Susan, is the Book of Mormon true?"

"Well, of course it is, Bishop."

"Do you love the Savior and do you believe in Heavenly Father?"

"Yes, I do."

"Is the prophet the head of the Church today?"

"Of course."

"Is this the true Church?"

"Of course it is. But I just can't stand the pressure."

I said, "Susan, will you be willing to try, because the Lord just gave you a promise."

She said, "Well, I guess I can try." That year she moved out of the ward and I lost track of her.

Well, at BYU in 1972, I volunteered to teach another religion class, besides the Book of Mormon, before going to my dental office. It was the Gospel Principles and Practices class. There were about sixty students in the class, and life was going just merrily along, and on the last day to drop the class, this student came up to me and he said, "I've got to drop your class."

I asked, "How come?"

He said, "Well, I'm on scholarship, and if I don't get a B or a B+ I could lose my scholarship; and I got a C+ on the test, and besides, I'm not a Mormon."

I looked at his little information sheet I had him fill out before class, and I'd missed it. He'd checked the "nonmember" box so close to the "member" box that I'd missed it.

I said, "Well, Jim, you mean you're just afraid you won't get a B?"

He said, "Well, how can I? I'm not a member and I just can't risk it."

I said, "Jim, I've got an idea. Do you normally study once a week for this class?"

He answered, "Yes."

I said, "Jim, I've got it. Would you mind studying with me Tuesday nights before Wednesday class for an hour?"

He said, "Yes, but what will that do?"

I continued, "Well, Jim, you want a B, right? Do you know who makes out the grade?"

He answered, "Well, you do."

I smiled. "That's right, Jim, I'm guaranteeing you a B or a B+."

"You mean you'll guaran . . ."

"I guarantee it. Look, I'm going to teach you extra Tuesday nights. If you're in my house for an hour, well, I'll make up the test too. I'll even help you prepare for the test. Jim, I'm guaranteeing you this."

Jim said, "Well, that's a deal, I'm going to study with you." So Jim came up to my house, and this went on for a couple of weeks, and then one day he asked, "Hey, Brother Ed, could I bring my brother and my roommate up? I mean, you and I have banana splits and root beer floats and doughnuts every study night; we might as well have parties when you teach."

And so I said, "You bet, you bring them up." So we went along for four more weeks, and then this one night they came up and they were kind of kidding around a lot, so I said, "You guys are sure having a hoot tonight. What's up around here?"

They looked at each other as if to say, "Okay, who's going to tell him?" and then Jim finally said, "Brother Ed, we've been thinking, and we talked to our bishop, and we all want to be baptized, and will you baptize us and confirm us members of the Church next week?"

As I floated down from the ceiling I said, "Yes Jim. I will, I will, I will." Well, his name was Jim Gerszewski, but I had mispronounced his name. Jim was Susan's brother; Susan was at the baptism, and joy was felt by all.

Now, you tell me that God our Father and Jesus Christ are not in charge of everything on this earth. How could those words come out of my mouth, "Your brothers will join the Church"? How, two years later, could one of those brothers be in my class? There were 20,000 students at BYU at the time. Don't tell me that the Lord's hand isn't in all things that are good. All three boys served missions. All three were married in the temple.

The Spirit "will show unto you all things what ye should do" (2 Ne. 32:5). Why is this so important? Because the vision in missionary work is that you must prepare people to feel the Spirit;

and their needs are individual—you've got to be in tune to what they need. Then, once they feel the Spirit, you can invite them to make a commitment.

That's what we called the commitment pattern. It's a pattern of showing love, and in the vision of the work, that's what we do. We show love. Teach by the Spirit, and people will want to make a change in their lives. We've all had the Spirit in our lives, and sometimes we don't recognize it and give credit to our Heavenly Father. In Doctrine and Covenants 11 we read, "Verily, verily, I say unto thee, put your trust in that Spirit which leadeth to do good" (v. 12). Have you ever had a desire to do good? Of course. That's the Spirit. "To do justly." Have you ever been honest in your dealings and just with your fellowmen? Of course. That's the Spirit. "To walk humbly." Have you ever been humbled? Of course you have. That's the Spirit. Have you ever made a righteous judgment? Of course you have. And of these the Lord says, "and this is my Spirit" (see D&C 11:12).

"Verily, verily, I say unto you, I will impart unto you of my Spirit, which shall enlighten your mind, which shall fill your soul with joy" (D&C 11:13). Every time a missionary preaches or teaches, every time you feel a good feeling, it is the Spirit. The Spirit is what makes missionary work successful. For without the Spirit, there is no conversion. So, the vision of the work is that we understand the power of the Spirit. You teach with that Spirit. You teach with that power to such a point that you have a power to convince men and women to come unto Christ because they feel that Spirit and act upon those feelings. You have the vision. You realize it's the Spirit that counts.

The Spirit fills our souls with joy in the vision. For instance, I would read the following account when I taught missionary preparation at the Orem Institute. Then we would give three cheers for each missionary who had received their call. We called it the "Brigham Young–Heber C. Kimball Cheer."

> September 14, President Brigham Young left his home at Montrose to start on the mission to England. He was so sick that he was unable to go to the Mississippi, a distance of thirty rods, without assistance. After he had crossed the river he rode behind Israel Barlow on his horse to my house, where he continued sick

until the eighteenth. He left his wife sick with a babe only three weeks old, and all his other children were sick and unable to wait upon each other. Not one soul of them was able to go to the well for a pail of water, and they were without a second suit on their backs, for the mob in Missouri had taken nearly all he had. On the seventeenth Sister Mary Ann Young got a boy to carry her up in his wagon to my house, that she might nurse and comfort Brother Brigham to the hour of starting.

September 18, Charles Hubbard sent his boy with a wagon and span of horses to my house; our trunks were put into the wagon by some brethren; I went to my . . . wife who was then shaking with a chill, having two children lying sick by her side; I embraced her and my children, and bade them farewell. My only well child was little Heber P., and it was with difficulty he would carry a couple of quarts of water at a time, to assist in quenching their thirst.

It was with difficulty we got into the wagon, and started down the hill about ten rods; it appeared to me as though my very inmost parts would melt within me at leaving my family in such a condition, as it were almost in the arms of death. I felt as though I could not endure it. I asked the teamster to stop, and said to Brother Brigham, "This is pretty tough, isn't it; let's rise up and give them a cheer." We arose, and swinging our hats three times over our heads, shouted: "Hurrah, hurrah for Israel." Vilate, hearing the noise, arose from her bed and came to the door. She had a smile on her face. Vilate and Mary Ann Young cried out to us: "Good-bye, God bless you." We returned the compliment, and then told the good driver to go ahead. After this I felt a spirit of joy and gratitude, having had the satisfaction of seeing my wife standing upon her feet, instead of leaving her in bed, knowing well that I should not see them again for two or three years.

(Orson F. Whitney, *Life of Heber C. Kimball*
[Salt Lake City: Kimball Family, 1888], 265–66.)

CONCLUSION

I have truly come to know the feeling of joy in the gospel, joy in preaching, and especially joy in others' success. I don't know if I can describe my feelings adequately, but I will try. I want so much for you to taste of the joys found in the gospel of Jesus Christ.

The joy of loving all mankind
   . . . the unlovable
   . . . the difficult companion, the prideful
   . . . the downtrodden
   . . . the haughty investigator, the unconcerned—
   . . . yea, love everyone unconditionally.
The joy of forgiving
   . . . those who speak evil of you
   . . . those who judge you unrighteously
   . . . those who reject you
   . . . those who disregard you
   . . . those who do not understand.
The joy of serving steadfastly and
   . . . knowing you are doing the will of God by enduring to
      the end
   . . . blessing your brothers and sisters
   . . . nurturing those who stand in need.

Finally, let me conclude with the words of a modern-day prophet: "I feel sorry for the man or the woman who has never experienced the sweet joy which comes to the missionary who proclaims the gospel of Jesus Christ, and brings honest souls to a knowledge of the truth, and who hears the expressions of gratitude and thanksgiving that come from the hearts of those who have been brought by his labor to a comprehension of life eternal" (Heber J. Grant, CR, Oct. 1907, 23).

It is up to you to become not just the missionary, but the devoted servant of the Lord who will live up to this message and this vision.

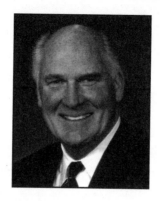

ABOUT THE AUTHOR

Brother Pinegar is a retired dentist and a long-time teacher of early-morning seminary as well as religion classes at Brigham Young University and the Orem Institute. He teaches at the Senior MTC and has served as a mission president in England and at the Missionary Training Center in Provo, Utah. He has been a bishop twice, has served as a temple sealer, and is currently serving as a stake president.

Brother Pinegar and his wife Patricia are the parents of eight children, and reside in Orem, Utah.